TRAINING IS BROKEN

Learning Doesn't Have to Fail

———

How AI, Autonomy, and Curiosity Activation
Will Replace Organizational Training as We Know It

Shaurav Sen

TRAINING IS BROKEN

shaurav.org

|Dubai|Washington D.C.|Singapore|New Delhi|
sen@shaurav.org
https://shaurav.org

Cover and page layout design by Miroslava Sobot

ISBN: 979-8-218-88142-9

For my father, Rajat Sen...

I learned from you that the strongest arguments are made with the clearest words and the deepest respect

"

*Not everything that is faced
can be changed, but nothing
can be changed until it is faced.*

———

James Baldwin

Author's Note

—

For more than three decades, I lived inside the consulting, learning, and development world—first as an entrepreneur, then as a researcher, consultant, provider, and later as a global executive. Across those years, a quiet tension followed me from project to project, program to program: the unmistakable sense that, despite all our effort and sophistication, something fundamental wasn't working. Learners were attending but not transforming. Organizations were investing but not seeing the outcomes they wanted.

When you're part of the system, you rarely name these things out loud. You optimize, you refine, you polish—*but you don't question the foundation*. I didn't either. Not fully. It's hard to challenge a structure while you're standing inside it. Only after stepping away from my traditional career almost a year ago, did I finally have the distance—and the *objectivity*—to assemble the observations that had been forming for decades. These essays may have been written recently, but their roots stretch across years of noticing the same patterns repeating themselves in different rooms, different companies, different continents.

These essays are *not* a critique of individual providers, facilitators, or practitioners. I've worked with extraordinary people across this industry—people who care deeply, work tirelessly, and genuinely want to help others grow. The problem is not the people. *It's the architecture they've inherited.* An architecture designed for a different era, built on assumptions we rarely examine, and defended long after the world around it has moved on.

My goal here is not to offer the next *guaranteed* solution. Nor is it to sell a new training system disguised as thought leadership. These essays serve a simple, yet different purpose: to raise the questions many have sensed but haven't had the space to articulate. Why do employees learn everywhere except in the programs designed for them? Why does so much training seem disconnected with real work? Why do our metrics reward activity instead of impact? And what becomes possible when AI exposes what was always true: that *people learn best when learning is personal, timely, emotional, and self-driven?*

If you are a leader, practitioner, or decision-maker who feels the status quo is no longer good enough—or maybe never was—I hope these essays give voice to your own quiet observations. I hope they provoke, unsettle, clarify, and spark new pathways for thinking about capability building and performance. You don't need to agree with every argument here. You're not meant to. *What matters is the conversation these essays make possible.*

This collection of essays is *not* a roadmap. It's an invitation—to rethink, to question, to let go, and to *reimagine learning* when we finally stop defending what no longer serves us.

~ *Shaurav*

HOW THIS BOOK WAS WRITTEN

This book was written using a combination of my own ideas, research, and observations accumulated over three decades as a consultant and practitioner—along with AI tools that helped accelerate the drafting and refinement process. AI didn't generate the concepts—it helped me articulate them more clearly, iterate faster, and refine my thinking. Think of it like working with an editor who never tires. All facts, claims, and conclusions remain my responsibility. I chose this approach *intentionally*—a book about how AI is reshaping learning should be created using those very tools. It would be disingenuous to advocate for AI-enabled learning while refusing to use AI myself. It would be equally disingenuous not to be transparent about it. The authorship is human. The tools are new. The responsibility for what you read is entirely mine.

Also, I am *not* an academic researcher or PhD. I have been a practitioner, watching what works, what fails, and what we keep pretending works. The ideas in this book aren't peer-reviewed research findings—they're simply observations and provocations born from *lived experience*. Consider them seeds for your own exploration. If something here resonates, experiment with it. If you can improve or refine these ideas, please share what you learn. We're all navigating *uncharted territory*. There's no perfect map for what AI makes possible—only the collective wisdom we build by trying, failing, and sharing honestly.

That's really the only way forward.

Table of Contents

Why We've Been Taught to Doubt Our Ability to Learn
We forget 90% within a week, yet spend $370 billion annually on programs with 12% application rates. Meanwhile, everyone knows how they actually learn: YouTube at midnight, AI at 2 AM, trial and error on real problems.

QUICK NAVIGATION GUIDE

If you're a CEO/CHRO wondering about ROI:
Start with Essays 1, 2, and 11

If you're an L&D leader facing budget pressures:
Focus on Essays 2, 3, and 10

If you're a training designer seeking better approaches:
Read Essays 7, 8, and 11

If you're skeptical about AI's impact:
Begin with Essays 1, 9, and 12

If you only have 30 minutes:
Read the Introduction and Essays 1, 7, and 12

If you want ammunition for change:
Essays 2, 4, and 10 provide the hardest-hitting critiques

If you're looking for solutions, not just problems:
Jump to Part III (Essays 7-9) and Essay 11

Note: Each essay includes a synopsis at the beginning and can be read independently. However, their full impact comes from understanding how these failures interconnect to create a system perfectly designed to prevent real learning.

INTRODUCTION

Setting the Context

A $370 Billion Question Nobody Wants to Ask

Here's an uncomfortable truth: We spend $370 billion globally on corporate training every year. Yet 70% of employees report they don't have the skills needed for their jobs. We forget 90% of what we learn in training within a week. Only 12% of learners apply new skills from training programs to their actual work.

These aren't opinions. They're documented facts from decades of research.

> So why do we keep doing the same thing, expecting different results?

This book is a collection of twelve provocative essays that challenge the fundamental assumptions of how we approach learning and development. It's not about tweaking the current system. It's about acknowledging that the system itself—built for an era of information scarcity—has become obsolete in an age where AI can provide personalized, instant, contextual learning to anyone, anywhere, at any time.

The essays you're about to read don't offer comfortable solutions. They expose uncomfortable truths. They question sacred cows. They challenge the very existence of practices we've accepted as "best" for decades.

This is not another guide to better training. This is a wake-up call for an industry that's perfected the art of looking productive while avoiding the harder question: *Does any of this actually work?*

Why These Essays, Why Now

Three forces are converging to make this the most critical moment in the history of corporate learning:

First, the traditional model has reached a breaking point.
Despite decades of innovation in learning technologies, methodologies, and frameworks, the fundamental metrics of success haven't budged. We're not getting better at helping people learn—we're just getting better at measuring our failure.

Second, artificial intelligence has eliminated information scarcity.
When anyone can access expert-level knowledge, personalized tutoring, and contextual guidance instantly through AI, the value proposition of scheduled, one-size-fits-all training collapses. The scarcity that justified traditional training no longer exists.

Third, the way humans actually learn has been exposed.
The pandemic forced us to see how people really acquire skills: through YouTube videos at midnight, AI conversations during problem-solving, peer discussions in Slack channels. Not through mandatory workshops and e-learning modules.

These essays explore what happens when we stop pretending the old model works and start building something aligned with how humans actually learn, especially in the age of AI.

Each essay tackles a different blind spot—from our obsession with measuring the wrong things, to our insistence on teaching at the wrong times, to our faith in experts who can't remember what it's like not to know.

Together, they paint a picture of an industry so invested in its own assumptions that it can't see they've become its biggest obstacles.

Why Am I Writing This: A View from Outside the System

After 32 years in the consulting and learning industry—as entrepreneur, customer, provider, and innovator—I stepped away. That distance provided clarity that proximity never could.

I didn't set out to revolutionize learning. But over the past three decades, I kept witnessing the same pattern: brilliant people, significant investments, sophisticated methodologies—and consistently mediocre results. The problem wasn't effort or intention. It was the fundamental assumptions underlying the entire enterprise.

My journey spans multiple perspectives:

- **As a start-up entrepreneur** (OnScreen), building an early learning platform showed me how technology couldn't fix pedagogical flaws

- **As a researcher & advisor** (Unilever, Corporate Executive Board (CEB), Gartner) studying best practices at world-class organizations revealed that even they struggled to transfer knowledge into action

- **As a global executive** (CEB, Korn Ferry, Mentora, Center for Creative Leadership) leading teams across continents demonstrated which interventions create lasting change versus temporary enthusiasm

- **As an innovator**, working with AI at the Center for Creative Leadership exposed how traditional training becomes obsolete when personalized learning is instant and free

Through 200+ workshops across the world and every level from frontline to C-suite, I've seen what works and what doesn't. More importantly, I've seen why we keep investing in approaches that don't work: because admitting failure would mean questioning an entire industry's reason for existence.

These essays represent observations accumulated over three decades, sharpened by conversations with hundreds of learning professionals and participants across cultures, industries, and contexts. They're not academic theories—they're patterns recognized through lived experience.

I share them now because the AI revolution makes this urgent. We're at an inflection point where continuing with traditional approaches isn't just ineffective—it's irresponsible. Organizations need honest, unfiltered perspectives on why their training investments fail and what might actually work.

Finally, these essays won't make me popular in the training industry. That's not the goal. The goal is to help organizations stop wasting billions on approaches that don't work and start building something that does.

Who Should Read This (And How to Use It)

SENIOR LEADERS AND L&D EXECUTIVES

If you're a CEO, CHRO, CLO, or L&D leader, these essays are written specifically for you. You're at a crossroads. The emergence of AI isn't just another trend to incorporate into your training strategy—it's an existential disruption that makes your current approach obsolete.

Many of you sense something is fundamentally wrong but struggle to articulate what. You see the investment, you see the activity, but you don't see the impact. You wonder if the problem is execution or if it's something deeper.

These essays provide language for what you're sensing. They offer frameworks for understanding why traditional approaches fail. Most importantly, they give you permission to question practices that have been treated as unquestionable.

LEARNING PROFESSIONALS

If you design, deliver, or manage learning experiences, these essays will challenge you. Some ideas might feel like attacks on your profession. They're not. They're invitations to evolve.

The future needs learning professionals more than ever—but not in the current form. We need curiosity architects, not content deliverers. We need those who can ignite learning, not just organize it. We need professionals who understand that their value isn't in what they know, but in their ability to help others discover.

How Organizations Should Use This book

FOR LEADERSHIP TEAMS:

- Share these essays before your next strategic review of L&D
- Use them to spark honest discussions about ROI and impact
- Challenge your team to identify which blind spots apply to your organization
- Ask the hard question: If we started from scratch, would we build what we have?

FOR L&D DEPARTMENTS:

- Make these essays required reading for your team
- Use them as discussion starters in your next offsite
- For each essay, ask: "Does this describe us? If so, what do we do about it?"
- Identify 2-3 essays most relevant to your immediate challenges and focus there

FOR INDIVIDUAL PROFESSIONALS:

- Read with an open mind, even when—especially when—it challenges your beliefs
- Ask yourself: Am I part of the problem or part of the solution?
- Consider how AI changes your role and value proposition
- Start experimenting with new approaches in small, safe ways

A Different Way to Read: Use Your AI Copilot!

These essays are quite detailed. It challenges decades of accepted practice. In our age of shortened attention spans, I realize many won't read every essay in detail.

> So here's an unconventional suggestion:
> **Use AI to help you navigate this content.**

Upload this book to your preferred AI assistant (ChatGPT, Claude, Gemini, Grok, or others) and engage with it differently. Here's a starter prompt you can copy and use:

"I've uploaded an book called 'The Death of Training: Learning Doesn't Have to Fail' that challenges traditional approaches to corporate learning. I'm a [YOUR ROLE] at a [YOUR INDUSTRY/COMPANY SIZE] organization.

Please help me navigate this content:

1. Which 3 essays would be most relevant to my role and context?
2. For each recommended essay, give me a 2-paragraph summary of the key argument and why it matters
3. What are the most controversial or challenging ideas that I should pay attention to?
4. Based on the essays, what 2-3 questions should I be asking about our current L&D approach?
5. If I only have 30 minutes, what sections should I focus on?
6. After reviewing my priorities, help me understand whether each essay contains genuinely new insights worth exploring or if it covers "familiar ground."

This isn't about avoiding the reading—it's about reading strategically, focusing your limited time on what matters most for your specific context.

A Guide to the Journey Ahead

This book is organized into four parts, each building on the previous to construct a complete picture of where we are, why we're failing, what actually works, and where we go from here.

PART I: THE SYSTEM IS BROKEN

We begin by exposing the fundamental flaws in how training is conceived, measured, and timed. These essays reveal an industry optimized for activity rather than impact.

PART II: WHY IT FAILS

Next, we examine the human factors—credibility, context, and expertise—that doom even well-designed programs. These essays explain why training that looks good on paper fails in practice.

PART III: WHAT ACTUALLY WORKS

Then, we explore alternative approaches aligned with how humans actually learn. These essays show what becomes possible when we stop forcing learning and start enabling it.

PART IV: THE PATH FORWARD

Finally, we imagine what learning could become if we had the courage to let go of what doesn't work. These essays point toward a future where learning is personal, contextual, and driven by genuine need rather than organizational schedules.

Each essay stands alone, but together they tell a larger story: the death of training as we know it, and the birth of something better.

Before You Begin

One final thought before you dive into these essays:

You might disagree with much of what you read. Good. These essays aren't meant to be comfortable. They're meant to make you think, question, and ultimately decide for yourself what needs to change.

Some ideas might seem extreme. Some critiques might feel unfair. Some suggestions might seem impossible given your constraints.

But ask yourself: If we keep doing what we're doing, where will we be in three years? Will traditional training even exist when AI can provide better, faster, more personalized learning for free?

The clock is ticking. The AI revolution isn't coming—it's here. The question isn't whether training will change, but whether you'll lead that change or be left behind by it.

These essays are my contribution to that conversation. What you do with them is up to you.

Welcome to the death of training as we know it.

And to the birth of what comes next.

Shaurav Sen
Dubai | Washington D.C. | Singapore | New Delhi
2026

PART

1

THE SYSTEM IS BROKEN

The Training Industrial Complex

Why We've Been Taught to Doubt Our Ability to Learn

It's time to stop treating adult learners like empty vessels waiting to be filled—and start acknowledging what we already know: learning is an individual sport.

SYNOPSIS:

We forget 70% of training content within 24 hours, yet spend $370 billion annually on programs that produce a 12% skill application rate. Meanwhile, we all know how we actually learn has changed: a YouTube video at midnight, a quick chat exchange with an AI tool, trial and error on real problems. The training industry has convinced us we're the problem when we don't complete their programs—but what if the programs themselves are the barrier? With AI making personalized learning instant and free, the role of structured education faces an existential crisis. The future isn't better content delivery—it's becoming activators of curiosity who create the spark that makes people decide they need to learn. Because once that spark ignites, nothing can stop them.

Here's a question that might make you uncomfortable: When was the last time something truly "stuck" from a full-day training session?

According to Ebbinghaus's Forgetting Curve (yes that's a real thing and that too by the same person who pioneered the Learning Curve!), we forget approximately 70% of new information within 24 hours if it's not reinforced. Within a week, that number climbs to 90%. Yet we continue to invest billions in multi-day training programs, wondering why nothing changes back at the desk.

> But here's the irony: *The L&D industry has convinced us this is our fault.*

We've been conditioned to believe that if we don't complete the long format full 8-hour training or the multi-day or multi-week learning journeys, if we don't sit through every module, then we are not serious about learning. We are the problem.

What if I told you that's backwards?

The Moment You Actually Decided to Learn Something

Think about the last skill you genuinely acquired. Not the one you were mandated to learn. I mean something you *actually* learned and can use today. Maybe it was finally figuring out how to increase your personal productivity, how to be more financially secure, learning enough about a new technology to have credible conversations, or developing a management or leadership skill that works with your difficult stakeholder.

> Now ask yourself: *Did you learn that by sitting through a three-day workshop?*

Or did you learn it through: a 7-minute YouTube video at 11 PM when you were stuck, or a conversation with a colleague who'd figured it out or after three failed attempts where you learned what *not* to do

The difference? You had **the spark.** You decided you needed to know this. And once you made that decision, nothing could stop you. You had access to the world's information—AI assistants, video tutorials, expert blogs—and you hunted down exactly what you needed, in the format that worked for you, at the moment you needed it. That's how most of us *really* learn.

The AI Revolution Makes This Crisis Urgent

Here's what makes clinging to traditional training models not just ineffective but borderline negligent: *The rapid proliferation of artificial intelligence and access to abundant knowledge.* We now have AI assistants that can explain complex concepts in exactly the way *you* need to hear them, generate examples tailored to *your* context, answer your questions at 2 AM, and adapt based on your learning style and pace. A working professional doesn't need to wait for next quarter's training— they can have a conversation with an AI that meets them exactly where they are. A student struggling with calculus can get explanations regenerated in different ways until something clicks, at their own pace, without judgment.

> *The world **has** shifted from information scarcity to abundance—and from one-size-fits-all to infinitely personalized learning.*

Yet we're still saying: "Sit in this room, at this time, and we'll deliver content in the way we've decided is best." Meanwhile, every learner has a personal AI tutor in their pocket that can outpace and out-personalize any pre-designed training program. This isn't just about corporate training. Universities face the same existential question: when students can get instant, personalized explanations from AI, what is the role of structured education?

The answer is to fundamentally rethink what learning means and what role we play in igniting it.

The Missing Ingredient: Emotion and the Activation of Curiosity

So, let's talk about what actually drives learning and change. True learning—the kind that leads to lasting behavior change—happens when emotions are engaged. Research in neuroscience is unambiguous: Emotion and cognition are inseparable in the learning process. No emotional engagement? No lasting memory. No lasting memory? No behavior change. Yet look at how we design most training: learning objectives, content delivery, comprehension tests, completion rates. *Where's the emotion? Where's the moment that makes someone care?*

We've professionalized learning to the point where we've sterilized it. We've made it safe, predictable, and utterly forgettable. Here's the uncomfortable truth: Our job is not to transfer knowledge. Information transfer is now free, instant, and infinitely available.

Our job is to become activators of curiosity.

We need to create the conditions where: Someone encounters an idea that challenges their assumptions...a question emerges that they can't stop thinking about...an internal motivation ignites that drives them to explore, experiment, and persist. Helping learners ignite the spark of "I *need to understand this*" is everything. Once that internal motivation takes over, the learner becomes unstoppable.

The Uncomfortable Truth About One-Size-Fits-All

Here's what the traditional training model refuses to acknowledge: *Every single person in that training room is different.* They have different prior knowledge, skill gaps, learning preferences, motivations, and contexts they'll apply this learning to. Yet we march them through the same content, at the same pace, in the same order, and expect the same outcomes. But acknowledging these differences is messy. It doesn't scale. So instead, we pretend the differences don't matter and blame individuals when training "doesn't stick."

Before the Pitchforks Come Out...

Let me be clear: I'm not advocating for the death of all structured training and coaching. Compliance training where everyone needs the same legal or safety information? Technical procedures where there's one correct way to operate equipment? Foundational knowledge where teams need a common language? One on one leadership coaching? These still have their place and often are the most optimal approach.

But let's stop pretending they're the right model for developing leadership capabilities for a group of aspiring or current leaders, driving behavior change, building strategic thinking, improving communication, or fostering innovation. These human, adaptive, contextual skills require something fundamentally different—something that respects the individual's journey and meets them where they are.

The Question Nobody Wants to Ask

What if the biggest barrier to learning in your organization isn't the lack of training programs—but the training programs themselves?

What if by trying to control, standardize, and scale learning, we're actually suffocating the very thing we're trying to ignite? What if instead of designing more engaging content, we need to fundamentally rethink our role? What if our job isn't to *teach* people but to create the conditions where they're inspired to teach themselves?

It's Time for Something Different

The future of learning isn't about better content delivery. It's not about more engaging videos or sophisticated LMS platforms. It's about fundamentally reimagining our role—*from knowledge transferers to curiosity architects.*

This isn't about abandoning structure or expertise. It's about respecting adults and young adults as the capable, self-directed learners they prove themselves to be every day when they're genuinely motivated. It's about lighting sparks, not filling vessels. It's about architecting curiosity, not transferring information. And in an AI-amplified world where personalized learning is the baseline expectation, organizations and institutions that don't make this shift will find themselves increasingly irrelevant.

Are we ready to let go of what's comfortable and explore what's actually effective and stop being the gatekeepers of knowledge and become the igniters of curiosity?

What's been your most powerful learning experience in the last year? Did it come from a formal training program, or somewhere else entirely? And more importantly, what triggered that moment when you decided you needed to learn it? I'm curious to hear your stories.

The Measurement Trap

Why What We Track Is Killing What Matters

We've become experts at measuring training activity. We've forgotten how to measure actual learning.

SYNOPSIS:

Training departments everywhere celebrate the same milestones: courses completed, attendance tracked, feedback collected, hours logged. Dashboards glow with upward-trending graphs that reassure executives their investment is paying off. But beneath this data-driven confidence lies an uncomfortable reality: we're measuring everything except the thing that matters. We've become masters at tracking activity while remaining willfully blind to outcome. The numbers tell us people showed up and clicked through—they don't tell us if anyone actually improved. This isn't just a reporting problem; it's a philosophical one. The metrics we choose don't just reflect our priorities—they shape them. When satisfaction scores drive design decisions and completion rates determine success, we've built a system optimized for looking busy rather than getting better. With AI now capable of tracking real performance improvement in real time, our addiction to vanity metrics isn't just outdated—it's becoming indefensible. The question isn't whether we can measure what matters. It's whether we're brave enough to look at what the data would reveal if we did.

The Dashboard Illusion

Every quarter, training teams present beautiful dashboards to leadership.

10,000 hours of training delivered. 95% completion rate. 4.7/5 average satisfaction. Engagement up 23% versus last year.

Executives nod. Budgets get renewed. Everyone feels vaguely reassured.

Then someone asks the only question that really matters:

"Did anyone actually get better at their job?"

Silence.

We've become extraordinarily sophisticated at measuring training *activity*. We've almost completely forgotten how to measure actual *learning*. Worse, we've built a measurement infrastructure that creates a comforting illusion of progress while systematically ignoring the one thing that justifies any of this: behavior change that improves real work.

What We Measure vs What Actually Matters

Look at what most L&D dashboards obsess over: Did people attend? Did they complete the modules? Did they like it? Did they pass the quiz? How long were they "engaged"?

Now compare that to what almost never shows up: Are they doing anything differently three months later? Can they apply the skill under pressure, in messy, political reality? Did performance on real work actually improve? Did key business outcomes move in the right direction? Would their manager say they're noticeably more capable?

We've known for decades this is the wrong balance. The Kirkpatrick Model—Reaction, Learning, Behavior, Results—has been around since 1959. In theory, it tells us to move beyond "Did they like it?" and "Did they pass?" toward "Did anything in the real world change?" In practice, we almost never get there.

A 2024 LinkedIn Workplace Learning Report found that while 77% of learning leaders say demonstrating impact on business goals is a top priority, only 18% are actually tracking the ROI of learning programs. The vast majority—over 90%—stop at satisfaction scores and completion rates.

Why? Because measuring satisfaction is easy. Measuring completion is easy. Measuring whether someone can actually do something better three months later is hard.

So we optimize for what we can measure easily—and then wonder why training doesn't drive results.

How Bad Metrics Create Bad Behavior

Metrics don't just describe reality. They shape it.

When we choose the wrong measures, we design the wrong experiences, reward the wrong behaviors, and then declare the wrong things "successful."

When completion is the goal — We make training mandatory and as frictionless as possible. People click through slides during meetings. They speed-watch videos at 2x. They memorize quiz answers. The metric goes up. The learning goes nowhere. Research by the NeuroLeadership Institute found that mandatory training is 50% less effective than voluntary learning, yet completion rates make mandatory training appear successful.

When satisfaction scores drive decisions — We optimize for entertainment, not transformation. We avoid discomfort, challenge, and honest feedback because they lower smile-sheet scores—even though they're often where the real learning lives. A 2018 study in the *Journal of Applied Psychology* found that learner satisfaction has almost no correlation with actual learning outcomes or transfer to job performance.

When time on platform is the proxy for impact — We pad content, stretch modules, and celebrate "hours of learning" as if time spent equals capability gained. As learning scientist Will Thalheimer notes, "Time spent does not equal time learned."

When quiz scores matter most — We test recall instead of application. We measure what's easy (definitions, multiple choice) rather than what actually matters (judgment under pressure, messy decision-making). The Association for Talent Development reports that knowledge retention drops to 10% within 90 days when learning isn't applied to real work.

Each of these metrics creates a system optimized for looking productive while avoiding the actual work of learning.

The Dangerous Illusion of Progress

Perhaps the most insidious aspect of our current measurement approach is how it creates a convincing illusion of progress.

Training dashboards look impressive. Executives see charts trending upward. L&D teams present evidence of "impact." Budgets get approved based on activity metrics that have almost nothing to do with whether anyone actually got better at their job.

This isn't just inefficient—it's actively harmful. It allows organizations to believe they're investing in capability development while that investment produces minimal return. It creates what researcher Laura Overton calls "the learning scrap heap": billions spent on training that never translates to performance.

The data on this is damning:

- Only 12% of learners apply new skills learned in training to their jobs (Saks & Burke, 2012)

- 70% of employees report they don't have mastery of skills needed for their jobs despite unprecedented access to training (Gartner, 2020)

- The training industry is valued at over $370 billion globally, yet most organizations struggle to demonstrate clear ROI (Training Industry Report, 2024)

- Less than 25% of respondents believe training measurably improved job performance (McKinsey, 2023)

Think about what this means: We've built a $370 billion industry that largely measures the wrong things, optimizes for the wrong outcomes, and then wonders why it can't prove its value.

The AI Revolution Makes This Crisis Urgent

In the age of AI, the measurement illusion becomes even more dangerous—and more obvious.

AI can provide real-time feedback on actual skill application. It can track progress on authentic work tasks. It can measure the gap between knowing and doing. It can identify exactly where someone gets stuck when applying knowledge under pressure.

Yet we're still measuring seat time and satisfaction scores.

When a knowledge worker asks ChatGPT how to analyze a dataset and then successfully completes the analysis, that's measurable learning and immediate application. When they sit through a data analytics workshop and pass a quiz, we measure completion—but have no idea if they can actually analyze data three weeks later.

The contrast couldn't be starker. AI-enabled learning *can* measure what matters: Did the person solve the problem? Did their work improve? Did they successfully transfer learning to a novel situation? Traditional training measurement systems *can't*—or more accurately, *won't*—because asking those questions would expose how little impact most training actually has.

What Would We Measure If We Actually Cared?

Here's the uncomfortable question that should haunt every training executive: If we actually measured behavior change and business impact, would most of our current training survive the scrutiny?

The evidence suggests: no. When only 12% of skills learned in training get applied on the job, that means 88% of what we're measuring as "success" is actually failure.

So what would we track if we genuinely cared about learning outcomes rather than training activity?

- **Time to competency on real tasks** — How long does it take someone to perform a skill independently and well in their actual work context? This matters far more than how long they spent in training.

- **Quality of work output** — Has the quality of their analyses, presentations, code, designs, or decisions measurably improved? This is what managers and clients actually care about.

- **Frequency of skill application** — Are they using the skill regularly in their work? Or did they take the training and never apply it? Frequency is a leading indicator of whether learning has transferred.

- **Performance improvement trajectory** — How are they progressing over weeks and months? Learning isn't an event—it's a trajectory. We should measure the curve, not just the initial completion.

- **Transfer to novel situations** — Can they apply what they learned to problems they haven't seen before? This is the true test of understanding versus mere memorization.

- **Manager-observed capability change** — Do the people who actually work with this person daily notice a meaningful difference in their capability? If not, what did the training accomplish?

None of these metrics fit neatly into an LMS dashboard. None of them are easy to automate. All of them matter infinitely more than completion rates.

The Choice We Face

The measurement trap isn't just about bad metrics. It's about using measurement to avoid a harder truth: that most corporate training doesn't work, and we've built an entire industry on pretending otherwise.

As long as we measure activity rather than outcomes, we can maintain the illusion. The moment we start measuring what actually matters— behavior change, performance improvement, business impact—the illusion collapses.

But we can't hide behind convenient metrics forever. The AI revolution is making the gap between activity and learning impossible to ignore. When learners can get personalized, just-in-time help that measurably improves their work, why would they sit through scheduled training that we can only prove they completed?

We have two paths forward:

We can continue measuring what's easy—completion rates, satisfaction scores, time on platform—and watch as our training becomes increasingly irrelevant compared to AI-enabled learning that actually changes behavior.

Or we can do the harder work of measuring what matters—behavior change, skill application, performance improvement—and redesigning our training to actually deliver those outcomes.

The first path preserves our budgets in the short term while making our profession obsolete in the long term.

The second path forces us to confront uncomfortable truths but gives us a chance to build something that actually works.

The choice seems obvious. Yet somehow, most of the industry keeps choosing the first path.

How much longer can we afford to measure the wrong things?

When you look at your organization's training metrics, what are they actually measuring? Completion or competency? Activity or learning? Participation or performance? And more importantly: if you measured what actually matters, what would the data reveal?

The Timing Paradox

*Why We Train People at
Exactly the Wrong Moment*

---

*We design learning calendars around
what's convenient for us, not what works for
those who need to learn—and then blame
learners when nothing sticks.*

SYNOPSIS:

We design learning around calendars, not moments of need. We send people to workshops months before they'll use the skill, flood them with content during onboarding, and roll out annual programs tied to budget cycles. Then we act surprised when nothing sticks. Cognitive science has told us for over a century that timing is everything: people retain more when learning is close to application and reinforced over time. The paradox? Organizations cling to scheduled training because it's administratively convenient, while employees quietly solve real problems through just-in-time, self-directed learning. In the age of AI, this gap becomes impossible to ignore. The question isn't "Can we time learning perfectly?" It's: *How much closer can we get—and what would it look like if timing was driven by work, not calendars?*

When the Moment Finally Arrives

In January, a new manager attends a three-day leadership program. She practices coaching conversations, learns a feedback model, and leaves with a thick workbook and a 4.8 satisfaction score. In July, she faces her first truly hard conversation. An employee is missing deadlines, the team is frustrated, and her own boss is asking pointed questions.

She freezes.

The models from January are gone. What she has instead is a racing heart and a browser tab: *"how to give tough feedback to defensive employee."*

She didn't need the training when it was delivered. She needs it *now*—when the stakes are real, emotions are high, and her brain is fully awake. That is the timing paradox in one scene: we schedule learning when it suits the organization; people need it when it collides with reality.

Just-in-Case vs Just-in-Time

Most corporate training runs on a just-in-case logic: teach this now, **just in case** it's needed one day. Front-load everything into onboarding, **just in case** it matters later. Run the workshop this quarter, **just in case** next year's budget is cut.

It shows up everywhere—annual compliance marathons that bear little resemblance to real ethical dilemmas, new-hire "bootcamps" that compress months of knowledge into a week, leadership programs scheduled around vendor calendars instead of role transitions.

On paper, this looks responsible: prepare people in advance. But human memory doesn't work that way.

The forgetting curve, first described by Hermann Ebbinghaus, shows that without reinforcement or use, we lose most new information in days or weeks. When you teach people something months before they need it, you are paying for them to forget.

By contrast, when learning occurs close to the moment of need and is spaced and reinforced over time, retention and transfer rise sharply. Modern research shows that spacing learning into multiple touchpoints and tying it to real work outcomes makes behavior change several times more likely than one-off events.

> **What** we teach matters, but **when** we teach may matter just as much.

The Reality Check: Perfect Timing Is Impossible

Here's the part we usually skip: it is *not* realistic to perfectly time training around every future challenge. You cannot predict the exact day someone will encounter their first performance crisis, when a deal will turn political, or when a safety issue will become real.

You also can't run your entire L&D function as an emergency response unit. Some disciplines—safety, compliance, core technical knowledge—require foundations. Some skills must be practiced before they're tested in the wild. This is why organizations retreat to the calendar—budget cycles are predictable, vendor availability is predictable, rooms and Zoom slots are predictable. Real work is not.

The problem isn't that timing is hard. The problem is that we rarely design for timing at all. We accept a crude compromise—"*everyone in Q2*"—and then blame learners when nothing sticks.

The goal is not perfection. It's to ask a different question: *If timing is a powerful lever, how much closer to the moment of need could we get with the tools and data we already have?*

How People Actually Learn at Work

Look at how employees really learn—the misalignment becomes obvious.

Recent analyses of workplace learning show repeating patterns: most employees prefer to learn **while they are working**, not in abstract offsites. Many want to learn **at their own pace**, in short bursts. A large share say they only want formal training **when it's truly necessary**—when a real task or problem forces the issue.

Yet employees still receive most of their formal learning in **large, infrequent chunks**—multi-hour sessions or long modules delivered a few times a year.

So they do the rational thing: when they get stuck, they search Google, YouTube, or Stack Overflow. They ping colleagues, scroll internal chats, or scan wikis. Increasingly, they turn to AI copilots for immediate help.

Quietly, employees have built a just-in-time learning ecosystem for themselves. Meanwhile, the organization congratulates itself on completions for programs nobody remembers.

The Hidden Costs of Getting Timing Wrong

Bad timing doesn't show up on the dashboard, but it shows up everywhere else.

1. **Wasted training spend**
   When someone attends training months before they need the skill, decay does its work. By the time application finally arrives, most of the investment has evaporated. Organizations then pay again—through refresher courses, coaching, or avoidable mistakes.

2. **Performance gaps during the "wait"**
   Between the moment a new challenge appears and the next
   scheduled program, people improvise. Sometimes that's healthy;
   often it is expensive—in rework, escalations, lost deals, or safety
   incidents.

3. **Time pulled away from meaningful work**
   Long workshops and e-learning marathons consume time that
   could have been spent solving real problems. When the content
   doesn't align with immediate challenges, that time becomes a
   sunk cost, not an investment.

4. **Learned dependency**
   Over-reliance on scheduled training teaches people to wait: wait
   for the course before trying the tool, wait for the program before
   having the conversation. Over time, this erodes self-directed
   learning and reinforces the idea that "real learning" only happens
   when L&D schedules it.

Where Organizations Are Getting Timing (More) Right

Some organizations are quietly experimenting with timing in smarter
ways.

In-app guidance instead of classroom training — Companies rolling
out tools like Salesforce use digital adoption platforms to embed
guidance directly into the system. Rather than asking people to
remember steps from a one-time class, help appears in the interface
when they're trying to perform the task. Result: faster onboarding,
fewer errors, better adoption—without extra "courses."

Learning moments inside collaboration tools — Enterprise platforms increasingly integrate into Microsoft Teams, Slack, and similar tools. Short videos, checklists, and scenarios surface when someone searches or clicks a help icon in the middle of real work.

Peer-powered help at the moment of need — Programs like Google's "Googler-to-Googler" (g2g) model make it easy for employees to tap colleagues for short, targeted learning sessions just when they need them—rather than waiting for the next formal offering.

None of these solve the timing paradox completely. But they represent a deliberate shift from training scheduled around topics to support aligned with **moments**.

A More Pragmatic Timing Strategy: Events, Signals, Choices

If perfect timing is impossible, what's the realistic alternative? Think in terms of three types of triggers.

1. **Event-based triggers** — moments you *can* predict: promotions or role transitions, reassignment to a new customer segment or region, rollout of a new system, product, or regulation.

   Instead of a generic "annual leadership program," align intensive support around the 90 days before and after a role change. Instead of a one-off three-hour tool training, design a short pre-launch primer plus in-app support for the first month of use. The timing isn't perfect, but it's far closer to reality than "same course for everyone in April."

2. **Signal-based triggers** — data points that suggest a need emerging right now: spikes in customer complaints around a particular issue, increased errors in a process or system, deals repeatedly stalling at the same sales stage, safety or quality metrics dipping in a specific site.

Modern systems already generate these signals. AI makes it easier to detect patterns and trigger targeted support: a short scenario, a checklist, a 10-minute clinic pushed to the teams experiencing the problem *this week*, not next quarter.

3. **Choice-based triggers** — moments when people self-declare need: searching the learning platform or knowledge base, asking "How do I...?" questions in chat tools, prompting AI assistants with specific tasks.

This is the purest form of good timing: the learner has felt the gap and is motivated to close it. If your ecosystem is designed so that these "help me" moments surface not just answers, but small practices, templates, and job aids, you're harnessing timing instead of fighting it.

What AI Actually Changes About Timing

AI doesn't magically fix timing, but it removes key constraints.

From courses to copilots — When AI is embedded inside the tools people use (CRM, office suites, code editors), help can appear at the exact moment of need. The system can answer "show me three ways to respond to this email" *inside* the email client, not two months earlier in a classroom.

From generic nudges to signal-driven prompts — Rather than blasting everyone with "learning reminders," AI can look at patterns of work and prompt learning where friction is highest: "You've had several tickets escalated for the same issue. Would you like a short scenario and checklist before your next call?"

From static paths to adaptive pacing — Traditional learning paths assume a fixed sequence and timeline. AI can adapt based on behavior: accelerating for those who demonstrate competence quickly, slowing down and adding practice for those who struggle—before they hit a high-stakes moment.

The technology is already here. What's missing in most organizations is a timing strategy that connects the pieces.

Where to Start Without Burning It All Down

You don't need to cancel your entire training calendar. But you do need to prove—to yourself and your stakeholders—that timing is a real lever, not a philosophical nicety.

Practical starting moves:

1. **Redesign one critical transition**
   Pick one high-stakes role step (e.g., new manager) and rebuild the experience around a 90-day window with short interventions, manager check-ins, and in-flow resources instead of a single big event.

2. **Instrument one important process**
   Choose a process where mistakes are costly. Use system data to see where people struggle and overlay just-in-time job aids, guidance, or AI prompts at those steps.

3. **Turn one content area into an AI-first experience**
   Take a topic like "difficult conversations" and design resources explicitly for use through AI tools: prompts, scenarios, and checklists that people pull *when they're preparing for a real conversation*, not weeks in advance.

4. **Track timing, not just completion**
   Begin capturing when people access resources relative to key events: before, during, or long after. Over time, you'll see in your own data that "closer to the moment" often means "more likely to stick."

The Real Question

The timing paradox exposes what corporate learning has really been optimized for: budget cycles, not brain cycles. Vendor availability, not learner readiness. Completions we can report, not capabilities people can use under pressure.

You will never control when life throws people into the deep end. But in a world where AI sits inside our daily tools, where data reveals where friction is rising, and where employees are already hacking their own just-in-time learning, pretending that timing is a minor detail is no longer credible.

The value of training has never resided in the workshop itself. It resides in the moment when what was learned meets a real problem that actually matters.

The question is not whether you can time everything perfectly. The question is: *How long are you willing to keep investing in learning experiences that arrive after the moment has passed—or long before it ever comes?*

PART
2
WHY IT FAILS

The Credibility Deficit

When Facilitators Have Never Done the Job

———

We've spent billions perfecting how to deliver learning. We forgot to ask if anyone believes the person delivering it.

SYNOPSIS:

Before a single slide is shown or framework explained, adult learners make a silent judgment that determines everything that follows: Does this person actually know what they're talking about? Not in theory—in practice. Have they carried the weight of the work they're now teaching? This invisible assessment, happening in the first moments of any learning experience, creates what might be corporate training's most expensive blind spot. We've engineered an entire profession around the assumption that facilitation skill and content knowledge can compensate for never having done the job. Decades of research on adult learning suggests they cannot. When learners doubt the messenger, knowledge transfer can drop by 40%—same material, same design, completely different outcome. Yet we've built training empires on professional facilitators who've never stood in the shoes of the people they're teaching. In an AI era where content delivery is commoditized, the one thing that remains irreplaceable is the credibility that comes only from scars. Some organizations are discovering their most valuable teachers may have already left the building—and are finding creative ways to bring them back.

The Question That Kills Learning Before It Starts

The moment a training session begins, participants are asking a silent question:

> *"Have you ever stood where I'm standing?"*

It's survival instinct. If the answer is "no," everything that follows becomes an uphill battle. People will smile, participate, and take notes. But a subtle emotional detachment forms that weakens every insight that follows. Because here's what decades of research confirms: **Adults don't learn from authority. They learn from credibility.** And credibility isn't built on delivery skills. It's built on the weight of lived experience.

Malcolm Knowles's foundational work on adult learning identified this: adults need to perceive the teacher as credible within their context. Without that perceived credibility, the brain's natural skepticism creates resistance—not to the content, but to the messenger.

A trainer who has never carried a quota cannot convincingly teach consultative selling. A trainer who has never navigated organizational politics cannot meaningfully teach influence. People instinctively know this. Their minds resist what their lived experience contradicts.

When Experience Is Missing, Curiosity Never Ignites

Real learning happens when something *matters*—when an idea feels grounded enough that it unsettles us, and curiosity forces us to lean forward. A facilitator without lived experience cannot create that moment. They can explain frameworks but cannot challenge assumptions or generate the productive tension that drives exploration.

What emerges instead is "ritual compliance"—the intelligent performance of learning. People complete exercises, say the right things in breakout rooms, and within 24 hours, 70% evaporates (Ebbinghaus). Not because the content was bad. Because it never felt real.

Research from the Corporate Leadership Council found that when learners question a trainer's credibility, knowledge transfer drops by up to 40%. Same content, different messenger, completely different results.

How We Built an Industry on a Faulty Foundation

The rise of the "professional facilitator" created a seductive belief: that content and context could be separated. Subject matter experts design, facilitators deliver, learners receive. Clean. Scalable. Efficient.

There's one problem: we don't learn from people who explain things well. We learn from people we find *believable*. And believability comes from scars, not certifications. A 2019 *Journal of Applied Psychology* study tested what predicts training transfer—content quality, instructional design, learner motivation, organizational support. The strongest predictor? Perceived source credibility: "the extent to which learners believe the trainer has direct experience doing the work they're teaching."

Yet most organizations treat facilitation skill as interchangeable with credibility. It is not.

What Credibility Actually Looks Like

Credible practitioners reshape the learning environment—not through charisma, but through *believability*. They don't just describe the model; they describe where it breaks. They share messy dilemmas from when decisions actually mattered:

- "I got this catastrophically wrong once. Here's what happened."
- "The framework suggests this, but here's where it falls apart in practice."

Participants lean in when they hear truth, not polish. Research from the Center for Creative Leadership found that experiences led by credible practitioners produce behavior change at rates 2-3 times higher than those led by facilitators without direct experience—even when content and format are identical.

The variable isn't the material. It's whether anyone believes the person delivering it.

What the AI Revolution
Makes Undeniable

Here's what makes the credibility deficit urgent: we now live in a world where information transfer is free, instant, and infinitely available. Anyone can ask an AI to explain any concept at any time. ChatGPT can generate examples, answer follow-up questions, and adapt explanations based on learning style—all at 2 AM, with infinite patience. So if your training's value proposition is "we'll explain things clearly," you're already obsolete.

What cannot be commoditized—what AI cannot replicate—is the credibility that comes from having lived the work. AI can explain a leadership framework. It cannot share what it felt like to use that framework during a crisis when the stakes were real and your decision affected people's livelihoods.

The future of learning is about people who can combine lived experience, reflective insight, emotional resonance, and the ability to provoke genuine curiosity. These cannot be templated or scaled through modules. They must be *earned*—through work, through mistakes, through pressure, through practice.

> As AI handles information transfer, *credibility becomes the irreplaceable human contribution to learning.*

What Some Organizations Are Starting to Explore

The uncomfortable truth? We've built most of our corporate learning around facilitation polish over lived credibility. We've chosen what scales over what works. But some organizations are beginning to experiment with a different approach—one that doesn't require choosing between credibility and scalability.

Tapping the Alumni and Retiree Pool

Companies like Boeing, McKinsey, and Microsoft have discovered that their most credible teachers may have already left the building. Boeing, for example, recruits engineers nearing or in retirement to guide younger employees through complex technical challenges. The result?

Knowledge transfer impossible to capture in documentation, delivered by people who carry the scars of doing the work.

Corporate alumni networks—once "nice to have"—are being reimagined as learning resources. Ninety-two percent of Fortune 500 companies now have formal alumni programs, increasingly including mentorship and knowledge-sharing.

The advantages:

No career competition — Retirees and alumni have no vested interest in politics. Participants can ask genuine questions without fear.

Authentic credibility — These are people who actually carried the quota, navigated the crisis. Their war stories aren't hypothetical.

Flexible engagement — Alumni can contribute without full-time constraints—workshops, projects, ongoing mentorship.

Cross-industry perspective — Tapping retirees from adjacent industries brings fresh views while maintaining relevant experience.

What This Could Look Like in Practice

Some organizations are experimenting with:

Targeted alumni facilitator programs — Identifying recently retired high performers and training them specifically in facilitation skills to complement their lived experience. The goal isn't to replace professional facilitators but to deploy credible practitioners where credibility matters most: leadership development, strategic thinking, complex problem-solving.

Virtual mentorship at scale — Using platforms like Zoom and AI-powered matching tools to connect current employees with alumni mentors based on specific challenges. A manager facing her first restructuring gets matched with an alum who led three.

That conversation happens in real-time, at the moment of need, not months earlier in a scheduled workshop.

Hybrid learning models — Professional facilitators handle program design, logistics, and foundational content. Alumni practitioners deliver the "here's what actually happens" components: case discussions, challenging conversations, messy scenario work.

AI-enhanced knowledge capture — Recording sessions with alumni experts and using AI to make that wisdom searchable and accessible. "Show me how Sarah handled pricing negotiations with difficult clients" becomes a query, not a training course.

The Obstacles Are Real But Solvable

This approach has challenges—alumni may lack facilitation skills, time, or interest. Coordination at scale feels complicated.

But consider: we've built multi-billion dollar industries around far more complex problems. The real obstacle is that we haven't prioritized credibility enough to solve for it. Organizations are addressing this through dedicated alumni platforms, light-touch facilitation training, flexible contribution models, and appropriate compensation structures.

A Starting Move: The Credibility Audit

Before building elaborate programs, start with one question: *For each of your critical learning interventions, does the person delivering it have meaningful lived experience in what they're teaching?*

If the answer is no, ask: *Who in our alumni network or retiree community could bring that credibility?*

Then pilot. Pick one high-stakes program—new manager development, strategic selling, innovation leadership—and test a credible practitioner model against your current approach. Measure not just satisfaction, but actual behavior change three months later.

The results might surprise you.

The Choice We Face

The measurement infrastructure we've built can't capture credibility. So we optimize for what we can measure—completion rates, satisfaction scores, facilitation polish—and then wonder why nothing sticks.

> *Does the person teaching this know what it feels like to do this job?*

If the answer is yes, training becomes possibility. It becomes the spark that sends people down a rabbit hole of self-directed exploration. If the answer is no, training becomes performance. It becomes compliance theater. It becomes one more thing that looked good in the slide deck but changed nothing in the real world.

We've prioritized what scales over what works. We've professionalized delivery at the expense of believability.

But we don't have to keep making that choice.

The organizations that will win won't be the ones with the most sophisticated LMS platforms. They'll be the ones who understand that **credibility is the new currency of learning.**

When you think about the most transformative learning experience of your career—the one that actually changed how you work—who led it? What made them credible in your eyes?

The Knowledge Transfer Fiction

———

Why Training Never Survives First Contact with Reality

We build perfect learning experiences for a world that doesn't exist. Then we wonder why nothing works when people face the world that does.

SYNOPSIS:

The workshop was flawless. Role-plays convincing. Feedback glowing. Then people returned to their desks and everything unraveled within hours. We've built a $370 billion industry on a fiction: that knowledge acquired in sterile environments transfers intact to messy, high-pressure workplaces. Research shows only 10-25% of training transfers to actual behavior—meaning 75-90% evaporates on contact with reality. Yet we keep designing as if the opposite were true. Some organizations are finally trying radically different approaches: embedding learning directly into workflow, abandoning case studies for real projects, using AI to deliver guidance at the moment of need. The question isn't whether knowledge transfer is hard—it's whether the way we've been doing it was ever going to work.

When the Illusion Shatters

A sales team just completed two days on consultative selling. The role-plays went brilliantly. Everyone practiced active listening, deeper questioning, resisting the urge to pitch too early. Evaluation scores averaged 4.7 out of 5.

Monday morning, first client call. The prospect mentions a challenge. The salesperson's brain lights up: "I have exactly the solution!" Before they realize it, they're pitching. Hard. The carefully practiced framework? Gone. The new questioning techniques? Forgotten.

They're back to their old pattern, selling the way they always have.

What happened? Nothing broke. This is working exactly as designed— designed for conditions that vanish the moment real pressure arrives. The training room had no quota pressure, no manager listening in, no competitor circling, no fear of losing the deal.

Reality has all of these things. And reality doesn't care what you learned last week.

The Gap Between Two Universes

We design learning for one universe and expect it to work in a completely different one. In training, you have time to think. At work, decisions happen in seconds. In training, scenarios are clean. At work, everything is ambiguous and emotionally charged. In training, mistakes are learning. At work, mistakes have costs. In training, you practice with people who are also practicing. At work, you're trying something new while everyone around you does what they've always done.

The gap is so wide that most knowledge can't survive the crossing.

The Three Foundational Errors

The knowledge transfer fiction rests on three assumptions that sound reasonable but collapse under examination.

ERROR #1: IF PEOPLE KNOW IT, THEY'LL DO IT

This might be the most expensive misunderstanding in corporate training. We believe that understanding drives behavior. It doesn't. A project manager knows she should delegate more. She genuinely believes it. She practiced it beautifully in training. But when she's behind schedule, when she knows she can do the task faster herself, when she's worried about quality—she does it herself. Again.

The knowledge didn't fail. *The situation overpowered it*. Behavior isn't primarily driven by what we know. It's driven by environmental cues, social norms, cognitive load, emotional state, and habit strength. Training addresses knowledge...*reality tests everything else*. Research in implementation science is clear: knowledge is necessary but catastrophically insufficient for behavior change. You need knowledge plus supportive environments, plus practice under realistic conditions, plus reinforcement over time, plus systems that make the new behavior easier than the old one.

Most training stops at knowledge. Then blames people when reality wins.

ERROR #2: INDIVIDUALS OWN TRANSFER

When training doesn't stick, we diagnose it as a learner problem. They're not motivated. They're resistant. They didn't take it seriously. This is organizational blame-shifting masquerading as analysis. Transfer failure is almost never about individual motivation. It's about systems that actively prevent application.

Managers who don't know what was taught, so they can't reinforce it. Worse, managers who explicitly contradict it: "That's nice, but here's how we actually do things." Peers who mock the new approach as naive. Tools and systems that make the old behavior faster and easier. Reward systems that continue to recognize people who demonstrate the opposite of what training taught. One study, for example, found that only 12% of training participants ever discussed applying the content with their manager.

The training isn't failing. The environment is killing it.

ERROR #3: EVENTS CREATE CHANGE

Perhaps the deepest fiction: that behavior change happens through discrete events rather than extended processes. We've known this is wrong for over a century. Ebbinghaus demonstrated that without reinforcement, we forget 70% of new information within 24 hours. Habit formation research shows that lasting behavioral change requires repeated practice over weeks. Implementation science confirms that sustainable change needs ongoing support, not one-time interventions.

Yet we keep designing training as standalone events. A workshop here. An e-learning module there. Then nothing for months. And we express genuine surprise when people revert to old behaviors within days. Events can and must ignite curiosity, shift perspective, introduce new concepts. But sparks without showing the learner how to make it relevant for themselves and keep learning and applying, will not create lasting impact.

We've built an industry that specializes in one-off events while ignoring the fuel entirely.

What Actually Works

Some organizations have stopped pretending and started designing for actual transfer. Microsoft embedded learning directly into Teams—guidance appears exactly when someone is about to have a feedback conversation. Application rates? Significantly higher than their old workshop-based approach—and, more importantly, sustained over time. This pattern mirrors what many 'learning in the flow of work' case studies report: when learning is embedded where work happens, people are far more likely to apply it. Not because the teaching improved—because the delivery aligned with how humans actually work.

Google discovered something counterintuitive: the more comprehensive the framework, the less it transfers. So they shifted to the smallest possible behavior change with disproportionate impact. Instead of ten delegation principles, one question: "Before starting any task, ask yourself—am I the only person who could do this?" Complexity impresses. Simplicity transfers.

LinkedIn found transfer success correlated almost perfectly with one variable: manager involvement. They added three manager touchpoints: before training (why this matters), during (identify applications), and after (three check-ins). Transfer rates tripled. The training didn't change. The environment did.

The pattern: *the problem isn't that we teach poorly. It's that we teach in universes too different from where behavior must actually happen.*

What AI Changes

AI doesn't solve knowledge transfer, but it makes the fiction impossible to maintain. When someone is stuck on a difficult email, AI provides guidance tailored to that situation—not vague memories from a six-month-old workshop. When a manager prepares for a performance conversation, AI offers just-in-time coaching for exact circumstances—not generic techniques recalled under stress.

AI can be present at moments of need in ways traditional training never could. It doesn't forget. It doesn't get tired. It doesn't require bridging the gap between abstract learning and specific application. This forces an uncomfortable question: if AI provides better support at the moment of need than people retain from training, what is training actually for? The answer might be: training's value shifts from knowledge transfer to reframing mental models, sparking curiosity, and activating self-driven learning to truly change. These matter. But they're not knowledge transfer. And we need to stop pretending they are.

Principles for Designing Beyond the Fiction

If knowledge transfer as traditionally conceived is fiction, what replaces it?

Design for environment, not just individual. Stop asking "how do we teach this better?" Start asking "what environmental changes would make this behavior the path of least resistance?" Training might teach a skill beautifully. But if the environment rewards the old behavior and punishes the new one, the environment wins. Always.

Reduce, don't add. When training doesn't transfer, the instinct is to add more. More practice. More follow-up. More reinforcement. This usually makes things worse. People under pressure have limited cognitive bandwidth. The question isn't "what else can we teach?" It's "what can they stop doing to make room for this new behavior?"

Make learning peripheral. The most effective learning increasingly happens around work, not separate from it. Embedded in tools. Available on-demand. Surfacing at moments of need. The best learning might be learning people don't even recognize as formal training.

Treat application as design problem, not motivation problem. When people don't apply what they learned, we default to motivational explanations. This is usually wrong. More often, the behavior is too complex to execute under stress, too time-consuming given their workload, too risky given team norms, or too unsupported by available systems. Fix the design, not the motivation.

The Uncomfortable Admission

Here's what the knowledge transfer fiction protects us from acknowledging: most training doesn't fail because we design it poorly. It fails because we design it for conditions that don't exist. We design for learners who have time and cognitive space. Real learners are drowning. We design for environments that support change. Real environments resist it. We design as if the gap between learning and application is small. It's enormous.

Until we acknowledge that gap—until we either bring learning to the moment of need or actively engineer work environments to support what we're asking people to do—we'll keep producing beautiful training that works perfectly until it encounters reality.

> The training isn't the problem. The fiction that training alone can bridge that gap is the problem.

The Expertise Trap

———

When Deep Knowledge Becomes the Enemy of Learning

The subject matter expert often makes the worst teacher. Not because they can't teach or don't care. Because they've forgotten what it's like not to know.

SYNOPSIS:

We assume expertise is the foundation of great teaching. It's actually an obstacle. The deeper someone's knowledge becomes, the more automatic their thinking grows, until they literally cannot access the cognitive steps that novices need most. This is the expertise trap: a cognitive blind spot where mastery erases memory of the learning journey. Research shows experts consistently overestimate what beginners understand, skip crucial intermediate steps, and communicate in ways that make perfect sense to themselves but confound learners. Unlike the credibility deficit—where trainers lack lived experience—the expertise trap strikes those who have the most experience. Their knowledge has become so compressed that they've lost conscious access to how they learned it. AI changes this dynamic completely. It doesn't suffer from the curse of knowledge and can break expertise into granular steps infinitely. The question isn't whether experts should teach. It's how we help them overcome the very expertise that makes them valuable.

The Paradox Nobody Talks About

> Here's the uncomfortable truth:
> the person most qualified to teach something
> is often the worst person to teach it.

A senior engineer who debugs complex systems in her sleep cannot remember what it felt like to stare at code that looked like hieroglyphics. A sales director who closes million-dollar deals through intuition has forgotten that negotiation tactics once seemed impossibly complex. They have mastered their craft so thoroughly that the knowledge has become automatic, unconscious, invisible. And that invisibility creates a chasm between expert and learner that no amount of goodwill can bridge.

This isn't the credibility deficit—where facilitators lack lived experience. The expertise trap afflicts those drowning in lived experience. They have the scars. They've done the work. But something strange happens on the journey to mastery: *the path you took becomes hidden from your own view.*

What Happens When Knowledge Becomes Invisible

In 1989, economists Colin Camerer, George Loewenstein, and Martin Weber coined the term "curse of knowledge" to describe a cognitive bias where informed individuals cannot accurately reconstruct what it's like to be uninformed. Once you know something, you cannot "un-know" it. You cannot return to the mental state of not knowing. The implications for learning are devastating.

When you first learn to drive, every action demands conscious attention. Check the mirror. Turn the key. Put your foot on the brake. Each step exists as a discrete, deliberate decision. But after years of driving, you execute hundreds of micro-decisions automatically while having a conversation and thinking about your afternoon meeting. The knowledge has compressed. The steps have disappeared.

Now imagine teaching someone to drive. An expert says, "Just ease into the intersection and merge smoothly when there's an opening." To them, this instruction is clear. To a novice, it's meaningless. When is there "an opening"? How do you "ease"? The expert has lost conscious access to the intermediate steps their brain processes automatically. They literally cannot tell you what they're doing because they're no longer aware they're doing it.

The Research Is Clear: Expertise Blind Spots

In a Stanford experiment, researcher Elizabeth Newton divided participants into "tappers" who tapped out well-known songs and "listeners" who tried to identify them. Tappers predicted 50% success. The actual rate? Three percent. The tappers could hear the melody in their heads. The listeners just heard random noise. The knowledge gap was so large that tappers couldn't imagine what it was like not to know.

The conclusion from decades of cognitive science research is unambiguous: *expertise fundamentally changes how your brain processes information, and these changes make it harder—not easier—to teach beginners.*

The Difference Between Having Experience and Teaching It

This is where the expertise trap diverges from the credibility deficit. Both create distance between teacher and learner, but in opposite ways: Essay 4 addressed trainers who lack the scars—they've never carried the weight of the work they're teaching. This essay addresses practitioners drowning in scars—they've done the work so thoroughly that their expertise has become invisible even to themselves. One fails because the teacher hasn't walked the path; the other fails because the teacher can no longer remember what walking that path for the first time actually felt like.

The *credibility deficit* occurs when the person teaching has never done the work. They can explain frameworks but cannot share the messy reality of application. Learners sense this lack and emotionally detach. The *expertise trap* occurs when the person teaching has done the work so thoroughly they've forgotten what it's like not to know how. They have more wisdom than they can consciously access. The teaching fails because that wisdom has become invisible to the teacher themselves.

One is a problem of too little experience. The other is a problem of too much—or more precisely, experience that has transformed into automated competence without conscious awareness. Both create the same outcome: training that doesn't connect. But they require *different solutions*.

Why We Keep Falling Into It

Organizations persist in equating subject matter expertise with teaching ability for understandable reasons. Who else would design sales training if not top salespeople? Who else would build technical certifications if not senior engineers? The logic seems airtight—right up until the moment the expert tries to explain something that has become automatic.

We've also built measurement systems that reinforce the trap. When evaluating training, we ask: "Is the content accurate?" "Does it reflect best practices?" We rarely ask: "Can a novice actually learn from this?" "Has the expert successfully decompressed their automated knowledge into learnable steps?"

> We optimize for expertise in the content while ignoring expertise in the teaching. Then we wonder why completion rates are high but behavior change is low.

How AI Transforms the Trap

Here's what changes everything: AI doesn't have the curse of knowledge. It hasn't traveled the learning journey, so it hasn't forgotten the steps. When an AI system teaches negotiation skills, it doesn't skip the part about managing emotional reactions because that process has become automatic—it never was automatic.

More importantly, AI can take an expert's compressed knowledge and decompress it infinitely. An expert might explain a concept one way. AI can generate fifty different explanations, each tailored to where a specific learner is stuck. It can identify the exact intermediate step a learner is missing and provide targeted support without the expert needing to consciously recall that step exists.

AI can also make expert thinking visible in ways experts cannot do themselves. By analyzing how experts solve problems, AI systems can surface the implicit decisions, the pattern recognition, the intuitive leaps that experts make unconsciously. Then it can break those into teachable steps. That's how IBM's Watson analyzes expert decision-making in medical diagnosis, identifying not just what experts conclude but how they got there—which symptoms they weighted heavily, what patterns they recognized, what possibilities they ruled out first.

This doesn't mean AI replaces expert teachers. It means AI can help experts overcome their own expertise. The combination—expert wisdom plus AI's ability to decompress and personalize it—creates something neither could achieve alone.

What Organizations Can Do Today

You don't need AI to start addressing the expertise trap:

Pair experts with instructional designers who aren't experts. Google discovered that the best training emerged when subject matter experts collaborated with designers who asked "stupid" questions. Those questions forced experts to unpack assumptions, articulate implicit steps, and translate jargon.

Conduct an "obviousness audit." For every critical learning program, have someone with zero background knowledge review the first hour of content. Every time they don't understand something, that's evidence of the expertise trap.

Record experts doing the actual work, not explaining it. When you record them actually working and capture their thinking out loud, you surface the hidden steps. That raw footage becomes training gold because it reveals what experts cannot consciously articulate.

Build "confusion catalogs" from learner questions. Track every question learners ask during training. Patterns emerge showing exactly where expert explanations disconnect from novice understanding.

Test training on people for whom it isn't designed. Before launching sales training for new hires, test it on engineers. If someone from outside the domain can follow the logic, you've successfully overcome the expertise trap.

Create "translation pairs"—expert plus recent learner. Instead of having experts develop training alone, pair each with someone who learned the skill within the past six months. The expert provides depth. The recent learner ensures clarity.

Use recent learners as co-teachers. Companies like Stripe involve employees who learned the skill within the past year to help design training. These "advanced novices" still remember the struggle points and the steps that experts skip.

The Hard Truth

The expertise trap is humbling because it reveals that the very thing that makes someone valuable—*deep mastery*—also makes them less capable of sharing that mastery. Your best engineer probably shouldn't design engineering onboarding alone. Your top salesperson likely needs help translating their intuitive brilliance into teachable steps.

> This doesn't mean experts shouldn't be involved in training: *it means we need to stop assuming that subject matter expertise equals teaching expertise.* They're different skills. Often inversely related.

The measurement infrastructure we've built can't capture this trap because it asks the wrong questions. "Is this expert-level content?" Yes. "Was it developed by someone with credentials?" Yes. But the question we should ask—"*Can someone who knows nothing learn from this?*"—rarely gets asked until after the training fails.

The Choice Before Us

We can continue pretending that expertise automatically translates into teaching ability. We can keep putting our most knowledgeable people in front of learners and wondering why the knowledge doesn't transfer. We can blame learners for not "getting it" when the real problem is that experts have forgotten what "getting it" requires.

Or we can acknowledge the trap and design around it. We can pair experts with people who bridge the gap. We can use technology to decompress automated knowledge. We can build systems that surface the invisible steps experts skip. We can measure not just whether training is accurate but whether it's learnable.

The organizations that thrive won't be the ones with the most expertise. They'll be the ones who figure out how to share that expertise despite the cognitive barriers mastery creates.

When you think about the best teacher you ever had, were they the person who knew the most? Or were they the person who remembered what it was like not to know, who could meet you where you were, who made complexity feel accessible? That's not an accident. That's someone who overcame the expertise trap—or never fell into it.

PART

3

WHAT ACTUALLY WORKS

Real Learning Begins When Teaching Ends

How unlocking curiosity—not curriculum— drives real transformation.

We dismiss "going down a rabbit hole" as distraction. It's actually where real learning happens—when curiosity takes over and people pursue answers because they need to, not because they're told to.

SYNOPSIS:
The phrase "going down a rabbit hole" is typically used pejoratively—a warning against distraction, a sign of losing focus, evidence of poor time management. But what if we have it backwards? What if the rabbit hole is exactly where transformative learning happens? When someone becomes genuinely curious about something, when a question lodges itself so deeply they can't stop exploring, when they look up from their screen at 2 AM realizing three hours have vanished—that's not distraction. That's learning in its purest form. The future of corporate learning isn't better content delivery or more engaging modules. It's becoming architects of curiosity who create the conditions where people stand at the edge of their own rabbit holes and decide to jump. Because once that internal drive ignites, nothing can stop them. And in the age of AI, where every answer is instantly available, the only question that matters is: What makes someone want to ask?

The Moment Everything Changed

Think about the last time you genuinely learned something complex—not because you had to, but because you couldn't help yourself.

Maybe you were renovating your house and suddenly needed to understand load-bearing walls. Or your teenager mentioned a historical event you'd never heard of, and you spent the evening tracing connections across Wikipedia. Or a colleague used a technical term in a meeting, and you found yourself three articles deep at midnight, following link after link, diagram after diagram.

You weren't completing modules. You weren't earning badges. You weren't checking off learning objectives. You were tumbling down a rabbit hole—and it felt entirely different from any formal training you'd ever experienced.

That difference isn't incidental. It's everything.

What Actually Happens
in the Rabbit Hole

When we dismiss someone as "*going down a rabbit hole,*" we're usually implying they've lost focus, wandered off task, gotten distracted by tangential curiosity. But neurologically, something powerful is happening that formal training rarely achieves.

Research in cognitive science shows that self-directed curiosity activates the brain's reward system—specifically the release of dopamine in the hippocampus, the region responsible for forming long-term memories. When you're curious, your brain doesn't just receive information passively; it actively hunts for it, creates stronger neural pathways, and retains it more durably. Studies by Dr. Matthias Gruber and colleagues at the University of California demonstrated that states of high curiosity enhance learning and memory for both the target information and incidental material encountered during that curious state.

More remarkably, curious learners show better retention not just immediately, but 24 hours later—precisely when most corporate training content has evaporated from participants' minds.

The rabbit hole works because *it flips the fundamental equation of learning*. In traditional training, we start with answers and hope people find them interesting enough to remember.

> In the rabbit hole, people start with questions they genuinely care about—and the answers become unavoidable.

The Training Model Was Built for the Wrong Era

Corporate training emerged in an era of information scarcity. Knowledge was expensive, difficult to access, and concentrated in experts, books, and institutions. If you wanted to learn project management, you needed someone to teach you. If you wanted to understand financial modeling, you attended a course. The training model made sense: gather people together, transfer knowledge from those who have it to those who don't, measure completion.

> *That world no longer exists.*

Today, any curious question can be answered in seconds. YouTube hosts millions of tutorials. AI can provide personalized explanations at any time, in any format, adapted to your level of understanding. The constraint isn't access to information—*it's the motivation to seek it out and the curiosity to keep exploring when you hit complexity.*

Yet our training infrastructure still operates as if it's 1985. We still design courses that "cover material." We still schedule learning at convenient times for the organization, not moments of genuine need. We still measure success by completion rather than by whether anyone cared enough to keep learning after the session ended.

We've optimized the delivery of answers while ignoring the more fundamental question:

What makes someone curious enough to seek those answers in the first place?

Why Mandated Learning Kills Curiosity

Here's an uncomfortable truth: *Making learning mandatory is the fastest way to ensure people don't actually learn.*

When you tell someone they must complete a training module, you've activated a psychological response researchers call "*controlled motivation*"—behavior driven by external pressure rather than internal interest. Studies in Self-Determination Theory, developed by Edward Deci and Richard Ryan over four decades, consistently show that controlled motivation produces shallow engagement, minimal retention, and rapid abandonment once the external pressure disappears.

By contrast, "**autonomous motivation**"—the drive that comes from genuine interest—produces deeper processing, better retention, greater transfer to novel situations, and continued learning long after any formal requirement ends. It's the difference between compliance and commitment. Between checking a box and actually caring.

The tragedy is that mandated training doesn't just fail to produce learning—it actively suppresses curiosity. When you force someone to sit through content they don't care about, you train them to associate "learning" with obligation, boredom, and coercion. *You make it less likely they'll seek out knowledge voluntarily in the future.*

> We've built a $370 billion industry around controlled motivation, then wondered why behavior doesn't change.

The Shift from Teaching to Igniting

If the rabbit hole is where real learning happens, then our role can't be to teach. It must be to ignite.

This isn't semantic wordplay. It's a fundamental *reconception* of what learning professionals do. Teaching implies transfer: I have knowledge; I give it to you. Igniting implies activation: I create conditions where you become curious enough to seek knowledge yourself.

What does igniting look like in practice?

It starts with questions, not answers. Research by Harvard's Project Zero found that the most effective learning experiences begin by provoking authentic questions that learners genuinely want to answer. Not rhetorical questions with obvious answers. Not "What do you think?"

followed immediately by "Let me tell you." *Real questions that unsettle assumptions, reveal gaps in understanding, or connect to challenges people actually face.*

Consider two approaches to teaching negotiation skills:

Traditional approach: "Today we'll cover the seven principles of effective negotiation. Principle one: Separate people from the problem..."

Igniting approach: "You're about to lose your best employee to a competitor. She's in your office right now. You have ten minutes. What do you say?" [Pause. Let them struggle.] "Interesting. Let's look at what just happened in your head..."

> The first delivers content. The second creates a need to know—*and that need is what sends people down the rabbit hole.*

The AI Revolution Makes This Urgent

In a world where AI can answer any factual question, explain any concept, and provide personalized tutoring on demand, what is the value of formal training that merely delivers information?

> *The uncomfortable answer: There isn't one.*

When someone can ask ChatGPT to explain a leadership framework, generate five examples relevant to their situation, adapt the explanation to their learning style, and answer follow-up questions indefinitely—why would they sit through a three-hour workshop covering the same material at a pace designed for the average participant?

They wouldn't. And increasingly, they don't.

But here's what AI cannot do: It cannot make you care. It cannot ignite curiosity about something you haven't thought to ask about. It cannot create the emotional spark that makes a question feel urgent and important. It cannot design an experience so provocative that you can't help but explore further.

That's the irreplaceable human contribution to learning: not delivering answers, *but creating the conditions where people decide they need them.*

What Organizations Can Do Differently

The shift from teaching to igniting doesn't require abandoning structure or expertise. It requires redesigning around curiosity rather than compliance.

Start with provocation, not objectives. Instead of learning objectives that list what participants will know by the end, design provocations that surface what they don't know but suddenly need to. Show them a decision point where their current mental models break down. Present them with a problem that's harder than it looks. Create cognitive dissonance that makes curiosity feel less like interest and more like necessity.

Make exploration the design. Rather than content followed by practice, reframe current mindsets or mental model to learners become naturally more inclined to explore. Use provocative data and anecdotes to engage learners at an emotional and personal level, not a linear path to follow that doesn't challenge their preconceptions. The messy process of hunting for answers, hitting dead ends, trying approaches that fail—that's not something to avoid. That's the rabbit hole. That's where learning happens.

Measure curiosity, not completion. Track how many people continue learning after the formal session ends. Monitor what questions they ask, what resources they seek out, what conversations they initiate. If your training successfully ignites curiosity, people will keep learning without you. If it doesn't, completion rates are just theater.

Build "curiosity infrastructure." Make it trivially easy for people to pursue questions when they arise. Embed AI assistants in daily tools so answers are seconds away, not next quarter's training calendar. Create channels where people can share what they're exploring and pull others into their rabbit holes. Recognize and celebrate people who go deep, not just those who complete requirements.

The Question That Changes Everything

The fundamental question of traditional training is: "How do we transfer this knowledge effectively?"

The fundamental question of *curiosity-driven learning* is: "*What would make someone care enough to seek this knowledge themselves?*"

The first question leads to better slides, more engaging videos, gamified modules. The second question leads to provocations, challenges, and experiences that people can't stop thinking about.

> *The first question produces compliance.*
> *The second produces commitment.*

The first question made sense when information was scarce. The second question is the only one that matters when information is abundant and AI makes every answer instantly accessible.

Standing at the Edge

The phrase *"rabbit hole"* comes from Lewis Carroll's *Alice's Adventures in Wonderland*—Alice sees a white rabbit, follows it out of curiosity, and tumbles into a world that transforms her understanding of everything.

That's not distraction. That's discovery.

The organizations that win in the age of AI won't be the ones with the best training content. They'll be the ones who understand that their job isn't to fill people with knowledge—it's to make people so curious they can't help but fill themselves.

They'll be the ones who design experiences that put people at the edge of rabbit holes and make jumping irresistible.

Because once someone starts falling, learning becomes unstoppable. The only question is:

What are we doing to make them want to jump?

Did you fall into the rabbit hole recently? Did it come from a formal training program, or somewhere else entirely? And more importantly, what triggered that moment when you decided you needed to dive in? What ways have you tried to ignite the spark in others? I'm curious to hear your stories.

The Complexity Delusion

———

How We've Made Simple Things Impossibly Hard

The training industry profits from complexity—200-slide decks, multi-week journeys, elaborate frameworks. Meanwhile, a 7-minute video changes more behavior than a 3-day workshop.

SYNOPSIS:

We've convinced ourselves that complexity equals rigor, that elaborate equals effective, that comprehensive means valuable. It's a delusion. Cognitive science is clear: complexity doesn't enhance learning—it destroys it. The human brain can hold roughly four chunks of information in working memory, yet we design programs demanding simultaneous processing of dozens of concepts. Meanwhile, transformative learning happens in elegant simplicity: a single reframing question, a 7-minute tutorial, one insight that shifts everything. Complexity persists because it serves everyone except learners—making vendors look sophisticated, justifying budgets, protecting trainers from vulnerability. In the age of AI, where personalized answers arrive instantly, training complexity isn't just ineffective—it's obsolete.

The Theater of Complexity

A vendor presents their new leadership program. The opening slide shows a framework diagram—circles within circles, arrows connecting boxes, colors coding dimensions. Forty-seven slides later, they're still explaining how the model works.

Everyone nods approvingly. It looks comprehensive. Sophisticated. Enterprise-grade.

> No one asks: *If it takes an hour to explain the framework, how will anyone remember it under pressure?*

This is the complexity delusion—the mistaken belief that elaborate equals valuable. We mistake complexity for sophistication when it's often just confusion wearing a suit.

Why Complexity Wins (Even Though It Doesn't Work)

Complexity persists because it serves powerful interests unrelated to learning:

Vendor economics demand it. A consulting firm cannot charge enterprise fees for simple advice. Simplicity doesn't justify the price tag. So they add modules, assessments, cohorts, and platforms until complexity matches the invoice.

Internal politics reward it. When a Chief Learning Officer presents to the board, simplicity reads as lightweight. "We're teaching managers to ask better questions" sounds thin. But "We've implemented a comprehensive, research-backed, multi-dimensional capability framework"—that sounds important. *Complexity becomes organizational theater.*

Psychological safety hides in it. There's profound insecurity in simplification. What if you strip something to its essence and people think it's too basic? Complexity feels safer—harder to attack because it is harder to understand. A 2019 study in *Nature Human Behavior* found people systematically undervalue simple solutions, perceiving them as less expert regardless of effectiveness.

The result: *an industry optimized for everyone except the person trying to learn.*

How Complexity Kills Learning

The brain science is unambiguous.

Cognitive overload shuts down processing. Working memory can hold approximately four chunks of information simultaneously—a fundamental constraint documented across decades of research. When training presents twelve concepts at once, the brain doesn't process more deeply. *It stops processing entirely.*

A 2019 meta-analysis in *Educational Psychology Review* examining cognitive load across 167 studies confirmed that instructional complexity beyond working memory capacity doesn't slow learning—it reverses it. People emerge more confused than when they started.

Transfer collapses under complexity. Research from the *Journal of Applied Psychology* (2021) found training complexity inversely correlates with application rates. The more steps in a framework, the less likely anyone uses any of them. *Not because they didn't learn it, but because complexity becomes unusable under pressure.*

Complexity triggers emotional shutdown. When something feels too big or abstract, the response isn't determination—it's *avoidance*. A 2020 study in *Neuropsychologia* showed cognitive overload activates the same neural stress response as physical threat. The brain shifts from learning mode to survival mode.

The Seduction of Elaborate Frameworks

The progression is predictable. Someone develops a useful four-step model. It works. Then enhancements begin.

First, nuance: "Between steps two and three, there's actually a critical interim phase..."

Then comprehensiveness: "We should add dimensions for stakeholder management, cultural context, risk mitigation..."

Before long, four steps have metastasized into a 47-component architecture requiring certification to understand.

This is framework inflation—the drift toward comprehensiveness that destroys usability. If your framework needs a framework to understand it, *it's not a framework—**it's theater***.

> People rarely abandon frameworks because they're too simple. They abandon them because they're too complex to remember when it matters.

Why Simplicity Creates Depth

Simplicity isn't the opposite of depth. *It's the path to it.*

Simplicity creates entry points. A single powerful question is easier to try than a nine-step process. Research from Stanford (2022) found that single, well-crafted provocations generated more sustained behavior change than comprehensive multi-week programs.

Simplicity accelerates iteration. Learning happens through feedback loops: try something, see results, adjust, try again. A manager who tries one new question in ten conversations this week learns more than one who plans to implement a complete framework next quarter.

Simplicity enables adaptation. Simple principles are moldable. People adapt them to context, combine them with other ideas, experiment with variations. Complexity demands fidelity—you must implement all components. This rigidity prevents the contextual adaptation essential for transfer.

Simplicity works with AI. When someone asks ChatGPT "How do I handle this difficult conversation?" *they get focused guidance immediately*. They don't want a comprehensive six-module framework. Research on AI-augmented decision-making suggests that simple, actionable prompts drive more real-world follow-through than complex, multi-step solutions—especially when guidance is delivered just in time through AI tools

Where Simplicity Already Wins

The evidence is everywhere—we just refuse to see it.

A junior employee searches Slack, finds a two-sentence explanation, and solves a problem a three-day workshop didn't address. A manager asks AI for "three questions before making a counteroffer," applies them immediately, and closes the deal. An engineer watches a seven-minute YouTube video and implements a solution—while the formal certification has a six-month waiting list.

Pattern: *When people have choice, they gravitate toward simplicity.* LinkedIn's 2024 Workplace Learning Report found that the most-consumed learning resources averaged under 8 minutes, while completion rates for multi-hour courses dropped below 15%.

Consider medicine—where mistakes kill. Research published in *The BMJ* (2020) analyzing surgical outcomes across 3,000 procedures found that simple checklists reduced major complications by 36%—outperforming years of complex training protocols.

> *Complexity persists only in systems that mandate consumption. Where choice exists, simplicity wins.*

The AI Shift Makes Complexity Obsolete

AI doesn't just favor simplicity—it makes complexity obsolete.

When learners can ask "What's the one thing I should focus on here?" and receive contextual answers in seconds, multi-module assessments become absurd. When AI breaks down any topic into digestible pieces, 200-slide decks become obstacles.

Traditional training's value proposition was: "We have comprehensive knowledge you lack." AI obliterates this. The new proposition must be: "We'll help you figure out what question to ask, create the spark that makes you curious, and build environments where learning from simple interventions is possible."

That requires the courage to be simple.

What Learners Actually Need

Strip away complexity and people need five things:

Clarity. What's the 20% that drives 80% of results?

Relevance. Why does this matter for me, with my specific challenges?

A single next step. What do I do in the next hour that makes a difference?

A spark. Something that makes me curious enough to explore further.

Permission to explore. Access to simple tools when curiosity strikes.

Notice what's missing: frameworks, phases, dimensions, architectures. None of those appear when you ask what learners actually need.

What Organizations Can Do Now

1. **Conduct a complexity audit.** For each program: If we could only keep 40% of this content, what would we keep? Delete the other 60%. Research from the NeuroLeadership Institute (2023) found that organizations reducing training content by half saw application rates double.

2. **Replace frameworks with principles.** Instead of nine-step processes, identify one or two core principles. Google's "10x thinking" principle drives more innovation than elaborate methodologies.

3. **Design "minimum viable learning."** What's the smallest intervention that could spark curiosity and enable a first attempt? Build that. Everything else is optional.

4. **Shift from coverage to momentum.** Stop asking "What should they know?" Start asking "What would make them curious to seek more?"

5. **Test with the "Tuesday morning" filter.** Would someone under normal Tuesday pressure remember and use this? If no, it's too complex.

The Uncomfortable Truth

Training doesn't fail because learners lack discipline. It fails because we bury simple truths under avoidable complexity—then blame people for not excavating them.

The complexity delusion protects everyone's interests except the learner's. Vendors maintain pricing. Learning departments demonstrate sophistication. Executives see evidence of investment. *But behavior change remains absent.*

In the age of AI, this becomes unsustainable. When anyone can access simple, personalized answers instantly, complexity isn't a feature—it's a bug. The truth beneath elaborate frameworks is usually simple. Often uncomfortably so. So simple that saying it feels vulnerable—what if people think that's all we've got?

But simple isn't simplistic. Simple is hard. Simple requires clarity about what truly matters. Simple demands courage to say "this is essential" and "this is not." Simple also has a unique property: *it actually works.*

When facing a real problem under real pressure—you don't reach for the 200-page framework. You reach for the simple truth you can remember and apply right now. Maybe that's what training should provide: Not comprehensive coverage of everything you might someday need, but the simple truth you need now, *delivered in a way that makes you curious to seek more when ready.*

That would require admitting that most of what we've built is far too complex to ever matter.

> The question isn't whether we can simplify.
> *It's whether we're brave enough to try.*

Did you learn something recently from a truly simple explanation or technique? Did it come from a formal training program, or somewhere else entirely? How have you explicitly tried to make your training as simple and short as necessary? I'm curious to hear your stories.

The Personalization Lie

———

Mass Training in the Age of Individual Learning

We call training "personalized" because it has a dropdown menu for industry. AI actually personalizes— to each person's context, gaps, pace, and goals. One is packaging. The other is transformation.

SYNOPSIS:
Every learning platform promises personalization. Adaptive pathways. Customized journeys. Tailored content. Look closer and you'll find the lie: most "personalization" means choosing your industry from a dropdown or selecting from three pre-designed paths. Real personalization means every learner gets exactly what they need, when they need it, at their pace, addressing their actual gaps in their specific context. What organizations deliver is personalization theater—mass-produced learning with cosmetic customization. Meanwhile, AI delivers genuine personalization effortlessly through conversation, adapting in real-time to how someone learns, what they struggle with, and what they need next. In an age where AI provides truly personalized learning instantly and freely, anything less isn't just inadequate—it's obsolete. The future belongs to organizations brave enough to stop pretending and start enabling conditions where real personalization emerges through learner agency and curiosity.

The Promise Everyone Makes

Open any learning technology vendor's website. The word appears everywhere: personalized.

"Personalized learning journeys." "Adaptive pathways." "Customized content for every learner."

Then you log in. The personalization reveals itself: a dropdown menu for your industry. A questionnaire placing you into one of four personas. A branching scenario where your answers determine which predetermined path you follow.

> *This isn't personalization. It's segmentation with better marketing.*

Why "Personalization" Became the Industry's Favorite Word

Every vendor claims personalization because the alternative—admitting you deliver the same content to everyone—is indefensible. But most personalization is surface-level by design:

The business reason: True personalization doesn't scale. Mass production is profitable. The solution? Create the appearance through minimal customization—industry dropdowns, optional modules, branching paths. You preserve economies of scale while checking the "personalized" box.

The political reason: "We've implemented personalized learning" sounds progressive in board presentations. It signals you understand people are different—even if your system treats them remarkably similarly.

The psychological reason: Simply labeling something "personalized" increases engagement. Research in *Journal of Marketing Research* (2022) found that personalization cues—even superficial ones—trigger psychological ownership, making people more likely to complete content regardless of actual relevance.

The result: *an industry built on promises it cannot keep.*

The Lie Exposed

Look at what passes for personalization:

"Personalized" means alternate versions exist—not that content adapts to you. You select "healthcare," so case studies mention hospitals instead of factories. But the framework, sequence, depth, and pace remain identical. Ten thousand people get the "healthcare version." That's not personalized—it's packaged.

Paths are predetermined by designers, not shaped by learner curiosity. Your assessment places you on Track B. But both tracks were designed months ago by people who've never met you, don't know your context, and cannot anticipate your actual struggles.

Timing remains pre-scheduled, not triggered by real need. The system might recommend Module 5 before Module 7, but it cannot know you're facing a difficult conversation tomorrow and need specific guidance right now.

Activities are identical; only the order changes. Adaptive platforms rearrange predetermined exercises. They cannot generate new activities matched to your emerging questions or the specific challenge keeping you up at night.

If ten thousand people receive the "personalized version," it isn't personalized—it's demographic targeting.

Why Real Personalization Is Hard

Yes it is hard and there is no magical fix. True personalization requires what traditional training cannot provide:

Deep contextual data. Not just your role, but your actual daily challenges, team dynamics, organizational culture, manager's style, upcoming projects, career aspirations.

Real-time understanding of skill gaps. Not generic assessment scores, but where you actually get stuck applying knowledge under pressure.

Precise timing alignment. Content arriving when you face the problem it addresses, not weeks before or after.

Emotional and motivational insight. Understanding whether you're curious or resistant, confident or anxious—and adapting accordingly.

Traditional training is structurally incapable of this. Even sophisticated adaptive platforms personalize only within their own content universe.

What Real Personalization Looks Like

Contrast two scenarios:

1. **Traditional "Personalized" Learning:** You complete an assessment. The system assigns you to "Emerging Leader Track." Over six weeks, you receive modules on delegation, feedback, and strategic thinking. The delegation module includes examples from your industry. You complete everything. Three months later, facing your first crisis as a manager, you cannot recall what the modules said.

2. **AI-Enabled Personalized Learning:** You're preparing for a difficult conversation with an underperforming team member. You ask an AI: "I have a one-on-one tomorrow with someone who consistently misses deadlines but gets defensive when I bring it up. What should I focus on?" The AI asks clarifying questions about your relationship, what you've tried before. It suggests one specific reframe and three questions. You try it. You follow up: "The conversation went okay but ended awkwardly—how do I follow up?" The AI adapts based on what just happened.

The difference isn't subtle. One delivers predetermined content wearing a "personalized" label. The other responds to your actual situation, in your language, at your moment of need.

Early work from Stanford's Human-Centered AI Institute and others suggests that conversational, context-specific AI guidance improves real-world application compared with traditional 'adaptive' pre-designed paths—*not because AI offers better content, but because it aligns to real context and timing.*

The Damage of Fake Personalization

When organizations claim personalization but deliver segmentation, consequences extend beyond ineffectiveness:

It undermines trust. Learners quickly recognize when something labeled "personalized" clearly isn't. The gap between promise and reality signals the organization either doesn't understand their needs or doesn't care.

It creates frustration. Nothing is more annoying than content claiming to be "for you" that clearly isn't. Each disconnect reinforces that the system doesn't actually see them.

It triggers disengagement. A 2023 study in *Computers & Education* found learners exposed to superficially "personalized" content showed lower engagement than those offered generic content honestly labeled as such. Fake personalization is worse than none—because it promises what it cannot deliver.

How Real Personalization Happens: Through Agency

Real personalization isn't something you deliver to people. It's something people create when given the right conditions.

Think about how you actually learn when you have choice. You encounter a problem that matters. You search for information specific to your situation. You explore at your own pace. You try something, see results, adjust, seek more guidance. You follow threads connecting to your unique context, interests, and goals.

That's personalized learning. And notice: it required zero personalization features from a platform. It emerged from your agency.

Essays 7 and 8 pointed toward this: Real learning begins when people decide what they need to know. Simplicity enables autonomy—the freedom to adapt ideas to your context. Personalization isn't a feature to build into training. It's what naturally happens when you remove barriers.

The AI-Enabled Future

AI doesn't just improve personalization
—*it redefines what's possible.*

AI becomes each learner's personal learning OS (operating system). Not a platform delivering content, but a conversational partner understanding your context, remembering your history, adapting to your style. It's a GPS that recalculates versus a printed map showing one route.

Organizations shift from assigning content to enabling exploration. L&D becomes context and curiosity architects—creating environments where learners explore freely, knowing AI will help navigate, fill gaps, and provide structure when needed.

Personalization happens through dialog, not content mapping. Old model: predict every possible need and create content for each. New model: learners articulate their actual need, and AI generates guidance specific to that situation. A 2024 MIT J-PAL report found organizations providing AI learning assistants saw personalization effectiveness improve 340% compared to traditional adaptive platforms—while reducing content development costs by 60%.

What Organizations Should Do Instead

Design "adaptive moments," not "adaptive modules." Create provocations surfacing real challenges, then provide AI-enabled tools for learners to explore solutions matched to their context.

Use AI-driven reflection instead of prescriptive activities. Rather than "Complete this delegation exercise," prompt: "Ask AI to help you think through an actual delegation opportunity you're facing this week."

Replace learning paths with choose-your-own-rabbit-hole experiences. Provide a starting provocation, essential principles, and access to AI guidance—then let learners explore. The path emerges from their curiosity.

Focus on contextual enablement, not content delivery. Ensure that when anyone faces a real challenge, they have simple access to guidance—whether AI, colleagues, or other resources.

Evaluate personalization by outcomes, not features. Stop counting "personalized pathways." Start measuring whether people get help matched to their actual needs when those needs arise.

The Courage to Stop Pretending

Most organizations know their "personalized learning" isn't genuinely personal. They know learners recognize the gap. But admitting it means confronting whether traditional infrastructure can survive.

It cannot.

When any employee can have a genuinely personalized conversation with AI about their specific challenge and receive immediately applicable guidance—for free, instantly—the pretense of personalization through dropdown menus becomes absurd.

The future doesn't belong to organizations with sophisticated adaptive algorithms for routing people through predetermined content. It belongs to those willing to admit that real *personalization requires giving up control*—letting learners drive their journey, ask their questions, set their pace, and follow their curiosity.

That's terrifying for an industry built on designing, delivering, and measuring predetermined experiences. Our role fundamentally changes from content creators to context architects, from path designers to enablers of exploration, from teachers to igniters of curiosity.

But it's the only honest path forward. Because personalization isn't something we do to learning. It's what learning becomes when we stop preventing it.

The question isn't whether your platform has personalization features. *It's whether you're ready to create conditions where genuine personalization—shaped by each learner's agency, context, and curiosity—can emerge.*

That requires letting go of the lie we've been telling. And building something true instead.

Have you recently gone through any truly personalized learning experiences? Are you trying to create something that's very different from what exists? Have you come across any powerful Ai features to help embed greater personalization and learning contextualization?

PART

4

THE PATH
FORWARD

The Captive Audience Fallacy

What Happens When Attendance Is Optional

Mandatory training creates the illusion of engagement. Make it optional and watch the truth emerge: most training wouldn't survive if people actually had a choice.

SYNOPSIS:

We've built an entire industry on captive audiences—people who attend training not because they want to, but because they must. Mandatory attendance creates the comforting illusion that training matters. Completion rates look healthy. Rooms fill up. Dashboards glow green. But strip away the requirement and most training collapses instantly. When attendance becomes optional, we discover an uncomfortable truth: the training we've spent billions developing holds so little perceived value that almost no one would choose it voluntarily. This isn't a learner problem—it's a relevance problem. In the age of AI, where genuinely valuable learning happens through voluntary exploration at 2 AM, the captive audience model isn't just outdated—it's revealing. Organizations clinging to mandatory training aren't ensuring learning; they're avoiding the market test that would expose which training actually delivers value and which exists only because we can force people to consume it.

The Illusion Mandatory Training Creates

Here's an exercise that makes training leaders uncomfortable: Take your flagship leadership program—the one with 95% completion rates and 4.6 satisfaction scores. Now make it optional. Completely optional. No manager pressure. No completion tracking. No "strongly encouraged."

What happens?

In most organizations, attendance drops 70-90% within months. The program that seemed essential when mandatory becomes invisible when optional. This isn't speculation—it's the pattern that emerges whenever organizations accidentally reveal training's true value proposition.

The captive audience fallacy is the belief that mandatory attendance reflects training value rather than organizational coercion. *We've confused compliance with commitment, attendance with interest, completion with learning*. We've built measurement systems that track whether people showed up while carefully avoiding the question of whether they would have shown up if given a choice.

What Mandatory Training Actually Produces

Research on motivation is unequivocal: controlled motivation—behavior driven by external pressure—produces dramatically different results than autonomous motivation—*behavior driven by genuine interest*.

Self-Determination Theory, developed over four decades by Edward Deci and Richard Ryan, shows that controlled motivation generates shallow processing, minimal retention, no voluntary continuation after pressure disappears, lower application to actual work, and resentment toward the activity itself.

By contrast, autonomous motivation—choosing to learn because you find it valuable—produces deeper engagement, better retention, higher transfer, and continued learning after formal requirements end.

A large meta-analysis of 200+ studies on autonomy-supportive teaching found substantially better motivation, engagement, and academic performance than controlling contexts—even when content was identical.

> When we mandate training, we're not just failing to motivate—*we're actively undermining the psychological conditions that enable real learning.*

The Truth Optional Attendance Reveals

Some organizations have experimented with making training optional, usually accidentally through poor enforcement rather than intentional design. The results are illuminating:

High-value training barely changes. Technical certifications needed for job advancement? Still full. Workshops solving immediate pain points? Still well-attended. Learning that connects directly to visible career or performance outcomes? People still show up.

Everything else collapses. Generic leadership development? Attendance drops 80%. Mandatory compliance training beyond legal minimums? Almost no one returns. Multi-week "learning journeys" without clear payoff? Evaporate.

The gap reveals what we've been avoiding: *most mandatory training exists because it cannot survive the market test of voluntary participation.* We mandate it not because it's essential but because it's not compelling enough for people to choose.

The AI Mirror

> AI makes the captive audience fallacy
> impossible to sustain.

When someone faces a genuine challenge—drafting a difficult email, preparing for a negotiation, debugging code—they don't wait for next quarter's mandatory workshop. They ask ChatGPT, Claude, or another AI assistant. They get personalized guidance instantly, adapted to their specific situation, at the exact moment of need.

That learning is entirely voluntary. No completion tracking. No manager pressure. No mandatory attendance. Yet people do it constantly—often late at night, because the need is real and the value is immediate.

This creates an uncomfortable comparison. Organizations mandate attendance at generic training people avoid when possible, while employees voluntarily engage with AI learning at 2 AM because it solves real problems. The contrast exposes what captive audience models have hidden: *when learning delivers genuine value, you don't need to force it.*

What Happens When We Stop Mandating

The few organizations bold enough to make significant training optional discover something unexpected: *learning doesn't collapse—it transforms*.

Attendance drops dramatically—at first. Programs that drew 500 people now get 50. Dashboards bleed red. Panic sets in.

But those who attend are different. They actually want to be there. They ask better questions. They engage more deeply. They apply what they learn because they came seeking solutions to problems they're actually facing.

Over time, word spreads about what works. Valuable training starts growing again through reputation rather than requirement. Programs that deliver real value rebuild attendance organically. Programs that don't? They disappear—as they should.

Microsoft experimented with this in their developer training. They made most technical workshops optional, expecting disaster. Instead, they found attendance at truly valuable workshops remained strong, participant engagement and satisfaction increased, application of skills to actual work improved significantly, feedback became more honest and actionable, and resources previously spent on low-value mandatory training redirected to high-value optional learning.

> The organization learned more about training effectiveness in six months of optional attendance than in years of mandatory participation.

The Question We're Afraid to Ask

If we made training optional, would anyone come?

That question terrifies training professionals because it threatens to expose what we've been avoiding: that much of what we've built wouldn't survive market forces. We've become dependent on mandatory attendance to create the appearance of value.

But here's the harder truth: *If people wouldn't choose your training voluntarily, you're not training them effectively even when you force them to attend.* Mandatory attendance doesn't solve the problem of low-value training—it just hides it behind completion metrics.

Building an Internal Training Marketplace

> The most radical solution is also the most obvious: let employees signal *what training they actually need.*

Rather than training departments deciding what everyone must consume, some progressive organizations are experimenting with demand-driven learning. They poll employees on critical topics, prioritize offerings based on actual interest, and let the internal "marketplace" determine what gets resourced and delivered.

This approach—sometimes called "*bottom-up training needs assessment*"—inverts the traditional model. Instead of pushing pre-determined content to captive audiences, it creates a pull system where training responds to genuine demand. Employees indicate what challenges they're facing, what skills they need to develop, and what topics would actually help them perform better. Training resources flow to what people actually want rather than what L&D thinks they should have.

The data supporting this approach is compelling. Research on bottom-up needs assessment shows it produces more accurate identification of skill gaps, higher engagement when training is delivered, better alignment between training content and actual job requirements, and stronger application of learned skills to work situations.

A marketplace model also creates natural accountability. Training that attracts voluntary participation proves its value. Training that doesn't? The market has spoken. Rather than forcing people through programs nobody wants while wondering why learning doesn't translate to performance, you discover immediately what's worth investing in and what isn't.

The resistance to this approach reveals the real fear: What if employees don't demand the training we've already built? What if the topics leadership thinks are important aren't what people actually need? What if our carefully designed competency frameworks don't match the problems people face daily?

> *These aren't arguments against marketplace thinking—they're evidence we need it.*

What Organizations Should Do Instead

Start with one experiment. Pick one non-compliance program currently mandatory. Make it optional for six months. Track not just attendance, but why people attend or don't.

Measure differently. Stop tracking completion rates. Start tracking: Would you recommend this to a colleague? Did you voluntarily seek more information afterward? Have you applied anything yet?

Design for voluntary attendance. Ask: "If this weren't mandatory, why would someone choose it?" If you can't answer compellingly, redesign until you can.

Poll for demand signals. Before building training, ask what people actually need. Let employees indicate topics they'd voluntarily attend. Prioritize based on genuine interest rather than assumed importance.

Be honest about what must be mandatory. Some training—legal compliance, safety procedures, required certifications—genuinely needs mandates. That's fine. But don't hide low-value training behind legitimate compliance needs.

Redirect resources freed by honesty. When optional attendance reveals programs nobody values, don't panic—celebrate. You've just freed resources to invest in learning people actually want.

The Path Forward

The future of corporate learning isn't better mandatory training—it's creating conditions where people voluntarily seek learning because it helps them do what they care about.

This requires courage. Making training optional means accepting feedback that mandatory systems hide. Some programs will fail. Some training professionals will need to develop different skills. Some sacred cows will be slaughtered.

But the alternative is continuing to force people through training that doesn't work, measuring success through compliance metrics that mean nothing, and wondering why learning never translates to performance improvement—all while employees voluntarily learn through AI and other channels that deliver actual value.

The captive audience model had a logic when information was scarce and alternatives were limited. In an age where anyone can access personalized learning instantly and freely, mandatory training looks increasingly like what it always was: *organizational theater that benefits everyone except the learner.*

The question isn't whether to abandon mandatory training entirely. It's whether we're brave enough to subject our training to the same market test every other tool faces: Would people choose this if they didn't have to?

> If the answer is no, we don't have an attendance problem. We have a value problem. And no amount of mandatory participation will fix that.

When was the last time you voluntarily sought out learning—at midnight, on a weekend, or during a crisis—because you genuinely needed it? Did it come from a mandatory training program, or somewhere else entirely? What would happen if all your organization's training had to compete for attention on that basis?

The L.I.Y. Method

Learn It Yourself: A Framework for the AI Age

The future isn't better content delivery—it's becoming architects of curiosity. A simple framework for creating 2-hour experiences that spark more learning than 2-week programs.

SYNOPSIS:
For decades, we've designed training as if our job is to transfer knowledge into people's heads. We've built elaborate programs, multi-week journeys, comprehensive frameworks—all optimized for coverage, completion, and control. Then we wonder why nothing sticks. The L.I.Y. Method (Learning Is Individual, You) offers a radically different approach: stop trying to teach everything and start igniting the curiosity that makes people teach themselves. Built around the SPARK Framework (Surface, Provoke, Activate, Reveal, Kick-start), this method compresses what matters into 2-hour "**SPARK Sessions**"—not to cover material, but to create the conditions where learners stand at the edge of their own rabbit holes and decide to jump. This isn't a scientifically validated solution backed by years of pilot studies. It's a practical framework born from three decades of watching what actually works, designed for an age where AI makes every answer instantly available but cannot create the spark that makes someone want to ask the question. The future belongs to organizations that stop measuring hours delivered and start measuring curiosity ignited.

The Uncomfortable Starting Point

Everything in this book has pointed toward one conclusion: traditional training doesn't work because it's built on the wrong foundation.

We've designed for *information transfer* in an age of *information abundance*. We've optimized for control when learning requires autonomy. We've measured activity when only behavior change matters. We've built comprehensive programs when simplicity transfers. We've promised personalization while delivering segmentation.

> The question becomes: *If we started from scratch, knowing what we know now, what would we build instead?*

The proposed L.I.Y. Method is one possible answer to that question. Not *the* answer—because there isn't one solution for every context. But *an* answer that emerged from 32 years of facilitating over 200 workshops, watching what actually creates lasting change, and recognizing patterns that consistently work across cultures, industries, and contexts.

This isn't offered as a scientifically validated methodology backed by randomized controlled trials. It's offered as a framework that addresses the failures documented in this book by fundamentally rethinking what learning professionals do.

What L.I.Y. Actually Means

L.I.Y. at its core stands for "Learning Is Individual, You" and not *Learn It Yourself* as in "figure it out alone." But as in: *learning is fundamentally individual.* You—the learner—are the only person who can make it happen. No trainer, no matter how skilled, can learn for you. No content, no matter how comprehensive, can substitute for your decision to engage.

This simple truth changes everything.

If learning is individual, then our job isn't to deliver content—it's to create conditions where individuals decide learning matters enough to pursue it themselves. If you are the only person who can make learning happen, then *our role isn't control—it's ignition.*

The L.I.Y. Method operates on five core principles:

1. **Curiosity is the only sustainable fuel.** External pressure produces compliance. Internal drive produces commitment. Our job is ignition, not instruction.

2. **Simplicity transfers; complexity doesn't.** The more elaborate the framework, the less likely anyone remembers it under pressure. Strip to essence.

3. **Timing trumps content.** The best teaching at the wrong moment fails. Adequate guidance at the moment of need succeeds. Design for moments, not modules.

4. **Agency beats assignment.** When people choose their path, they own the outcome. When you assign it, they rent attention until the requirement ends.

5. **AI changes everything.** In an age where any question gets instant answers, our value isn't information—it's inspiration. We don't teach content; we architect curiosity.

The Three Confluences Required for Self-Motivated Learning

Through my observations and research looking at self-reported learning breakthroughs—moments when people described experiencing genuine, sustained learning that led to real behavior change—I identified a consistent pattern. True learning, the kind that results in lasting change, occurs when three specific elements converge within a compressed timeframe:

Confluence #1: DISRUPTION – *disruption* is the realization that the current approach isn't working or isn't optimal. It's the moment when existing assumptions are challenged, when mental models are questioned, when people recognize that their current way of thinking or doing things is insufficient or outdated.

Confluence #2: URGENCY – *urgency* is the emotional recognition that inaction has real, personal costs. It moves beyond intellectual understanding to emotional discomfort with the status quo. Urgency answers the question "Why should I care?" and more specifically, "Why should I care enough to do something about this now?"

Confluence #3: POSSIBILITY – *possibility* is the "aha moment" that reveals a different path forward. It's the realization that "there's another way" combined with evidence that this way actually works. Possibility provides hope that change is not just necessary (disruption + urgency) but actually achievable.

The SPARK Framework: How It Works

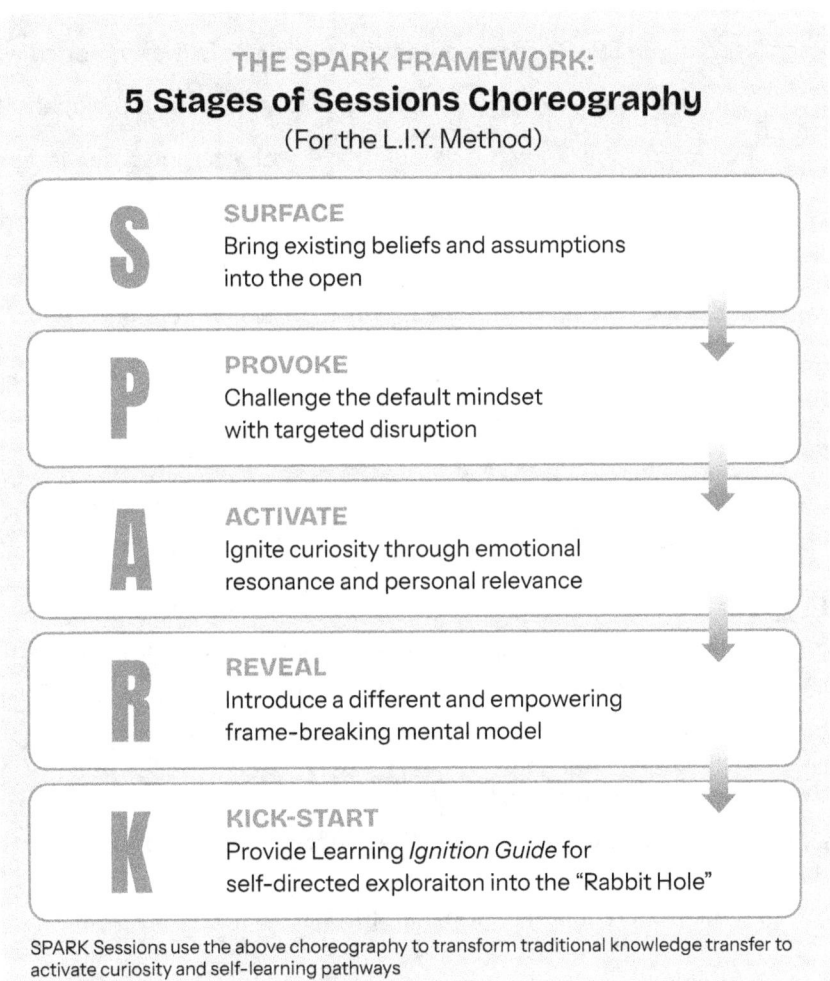

THE SPARK FRAMEWORK:
5 Stages of Sessions Choreography
(For the L.I.Y. Method)

S — SURFACE
Bring existing beliefs and assumptions into the open

P — PROVOKE
Challenge the default mindset with targeted disruption

A — ACTIVATE
Ignite curiosity through emotional resonance and personal relevance

R — REVEAL
Introduce a different and empowering frame-breaking mental model

K — KICK-START
Provide Learning *Ignition Guide* for self-directed exploraiton into the "Rabbit Hole"

SPARK Sessions use the above choreography to transform traditional knowledge transfer to activate curiosity and self-learning pathways

The SPARK Framework is the operational heart of the L.I.Y. Method. It's designed to create what I call "**SPARK Sessions**"—compressed 2-hour experiences akin to a "*Sparkshop*" that ignite more learning than traditional multi-day programs. Even shorter formats are shared in a separate whitepaper: from 5-minute "SparkPlug" to a 30-minute SparkPod.

The name matters: not workshops (where we work through material), but SPARK Sessions (where we ignite the spark that sends people exploring on their own).

Each letter of the SPARK represents a *distinct phase* in the session flow:

1. **Surface** – Bring existing beliefs and assumptions into the open
2. **Provoke** – Challenge the default frame with a targeted disruption
3. **Activate** – Create emotional relevance and personal resonance
4. **Reveal** – Introduce a clearer, more empowering mental model
5. **Kickstart** – Provide the immediate path for self-directed exploration

This sequence creates the arc of recognition → disruption → emotional ignition → possibility → momentum. Below is the detailed breakdown of each stage.

STAGE 1: S - SURFACE

Purpose
Expose existing assumptions, beliefs, and prior knowledge—without judgment—so participants feel seen and psychologically safe before being challenged.

Why This Stage Matters
Learners reject new ideas when they feel misunderstood. Surface dissolves defensiveness by validating participants' starting point and building the trust required for meaningful disruption.

Key Activities
- Simple prompts ("Define X in one sentence")
- Polls that reveal common assumptions
- Brief facilitator acknowledgment of shared beliefs
- Light narrative demonstrating similar starting points

STAGE 2: **P - PROVOKE**

Purpose

Introduce a surprising insight, contradiction, or counterintuitive example that destabilizes the default way of thinking.

Why This Stage Matters

Provocation creates cognitive dissonance—the spark that shifts the learner from passive listening to active questioning.

Key Activities

- Contradictory data
- Unexpected demonstrations
- "What if your assumption is backwards?" questions
- Old vs. new model contrasts

STAGE 3: **A - ACTIVATE**

Purpose

Translate intellectual disruption into emotional relevance—urgency, curiosity, surprise, or discomfort.

Why This Stage Matters

We learn when we feel. Emotional activation creates the internal shift required to pursue answers independently after the session.

Key Activities

- Personal impact scenarios
- Short stories revealing hidden consequences
- Reflection exercises surfacing emotional patterns
- Future-self thought experiments

STAGE 4: R - REVEAL

Purpose

Present a reimagined frame or mental model that resolves the earlier tension and unlocks a new way of understanding the topic.

Why This Stage Matters

After provocation and emotional ignition, learners need clarity and possibility—not dense content. Reveal provides the "aha" that reorganizes their thinking.

Key Activities

- Clean diagram or framework
- Before/after reframing
- Simple principle explaining a complex issue
- Examples of the new model in action

STAGE 5: K - KICKSTART

Purpose

Convert momentum into action by removing friction and handing the learner a clear path for immediate next steps.

Why This Stage Matters

Curiosity fades quickly unless directed. Kickstart ensures the learner leaves with both energy and direction.

Key Activities

- Quick-start task
- 24-hour follow-up micro-action
- AI prompts for deeper exploration
- Learning Ignition Guide (short starter kit of curated resources)

This is where the rabbit hole begins. The SPARK Session doesn't try to teach everything—it creates enough curiosity that participants cannot help but keep learning.

EXAMPLE:
SPARK Framework Comes Alive in a Financial Literacy/Wellness Topic on "What is Money"

Surface

Participants attempt to define money. Responses expose ambiguity, emotional associations, and contradictory beliefs—setting the stage for disruption.

Provoke

The facilitator presents a shell, gold coin, banknote, mobile banking app, and Bitcoin QR code:
"Which of these is money—and why?"
The contradiction destabilizes the belief that money's power comes from physical form.

Activate

A narrative illustrates two people with identical incomes making opposite financial decisions based on different "money stories." Participants suddenly see their own patterns—fear, guilt, impulse, scarcity—in a new light.

Reveal

Money is reframed as **stored human energy and time**, not a physical object. This opens up an entirely new way to interpret:

- inflation as energy leakage
- investing as energy multiplication
- spending as energy conversion
- saving as energy storage

Kickstart

Participants receive a Money Ignition Guide containing:

- a personal money story reflection
- curated resources on money psychology
- prompts for designing a new money identity
- a 10-minute micro-action: "Rewrite your definition of money and revise one financial behavior accordingly."

Why This Works in the AI Age

The L.I.Y. Method isn't fighting against AI—it's designed for a world where AI exists.

When participants leave a SPARK Session with questions they're genuinely curious about, AI becomes their personalized learning engine. They can ask follow-up questions, explore edge cases, adapt principles to their context—all at their own pace, matched to their actual needs. Early evidence suggests that experiences which trigger genuine curiosity drive significantly greater sustained engagement than content-first teaching models

The SPARK Session creates the spark.
AI fuels the journey down the rabbit hole.

What Organizations Can Do

Implementing the L.I.Y. Method means fundamentally rethinking learning design:

- **Replace multi-day programs with SPARK Sessions.** A well-designed 2- hour SPARK Session followed by AI-enabled exploration produces more behavior change than a three-day workshop.

- **Design backward from the spark, not forward from content.** Don't ask "What do they need to know?" Ask "What would make them desperately curious to know more?"

- **Measure curiosity ignited, not completion achieved.** Track questions asked, resources explored, conversations initiated, applications attempted. These indicate whether the spark caught.

- **Enable AI-powered follow-through.** Provide prompts, frameworks, and tools that make it trivially easy for participants to continue learning through AI conversations matched to their specific context.

- **Abandon comprehensiveness.** You cannot cover everything in 2-3 hours. You don't need to. Cover the 20% that creates 80% of the curiosity, then enable self-directed exploration of the rest.

Limitations and Caveats

This framework isn't magic, and it isn't universally applicable.

- **It requires skilled facilitation.** Surfacing mental models without judgment, provoking without alienating, activating meaningfully—these demand facilitator capability. This method makes facilitation harder, not easier.

- **It doesn't work for compliance training.** When everyone must receive identical information for regulatory reasons, SPARK Sessions aren't appropriate. Some contexts genuinely require standardized content delivery.

- **It demands organizational support.** If participants return to environments hostile to trying new approaches, curiosity dies. The method requires managers who support experimentation and cultures that tolerate productive failure.

- **It's harder to measure traditionally.** You can't easily prove ROI through completion rates and test scores. Measuring curiosity and sustained learning requires different metrics and longer timeframes.

- **It hasn't been validated through rigorous research trials.** This framework emerged from practice, refined through iteration, informed by research—but it hasn't undergone the randomized controlled trials that would constitute scientific validation.

What it has is 30+ years of pattern recognition across hundreds of implementations, supported by research on curiosity, motivation, cognitive load, and learning transfer. It's offered not as proven truth, but as practical wisdom worth considering.

The Real Test

The L.I.Y. Method will be judged not by whether it's theoretically sound, but by whether it produces different results.

If organizations implement SPARK Sessions and participants don't continue learning afterward—if curiosity doesn't ignite, if rabbit holes remain unexplored, if behavior doesn't change—then the method fails regardless of how elegant the framework appears.

But if participants leave thinking "I need to understand this better," if they engage with AI to explore deeper, if they try new approaches and report back on what worked, if learning becomes something they drive rather than something done to them—then perhaps this approach offers one path forward.

The ultimate question isn't whether the L.I.Y. Method is right. It's whether continuing with approaches we know don't work is defensible.

The choice is stark: Keep building comprehensive programs that produce 12% application rates, or experiment with compressed experiences designed to ignite the curiosity that AI can fuel.

> One preserves what we've always done.
> The other admits we need something different.

Which will you choose?

The Learning Revolution

————

What Happens When We Finally Let Go

When the way we've always done things stops working, we get one choice: protect the system— or protect the people it was supposed to serve. The AI era is forcing that decision faster than most leaders are comfortable admitting.

SYNOPSIS

For decades, we've optimized corporate learning around control: fixed curricula, mandatory attendance, standardized content, centralized platforms. That logic made sense in an era of information scarcity. It is fatal in an era where every employee carries a personal AI tutor in their pocket. The Learning Revolution is not about adding more digital content, smarter LMS features, or "AI-enhanced" versions of the same old programs. It's about a clean break: accepting that training-as-we-know-it has reached the end of its useful life, and choosing to build something aligned with how humans actually learn in an AI-amplified world. This is a manifesto for leaders willing to stop protecting sunk costs and start protecting future relevance—by letting go of control, rethinking their role, and redesigning learning as a voluntary, emotionally charged, AI-enabled ecosystem that serves real work instead of legacy structures.

The Fork in the Road

> Every system faces a moment when its internal logic stops matching reality.
> For corporate learning, that moment is now.

On one side: training as scheduled events, learning as content delivery, engagement as attendance, measurement as dashboards that glow green while performance stalls. On the other side: how people actually learn today. A question at 10:47 PM. A conversation with AI at 2:13 AM. A three-minute clip, a colleague's workaround, a quick experiment on a live problem.

Seventy percent of training content is forgotten within a week. Fewer than 25% of participants apply what they learned. The $370 billion industry produces measurable behavior change in roughly one out of eight people.

These aren't contested numbers. They're quietly acknowledged at every industry conference. Yet we keep building. More modules. Better platforms. As if the problem were insufficient innovation rather than fundamental misdirection.

The revolution isn't about doing training better. It's about recognizing the entire premise was always wrong: that learning happens through structured content delivery to groups at scheduled times.

We just had no alternative. Now we do.

Three Non-Negotiable Realities

1. **The current system doesn't work at scale.** Application rates hover in the low teens. Employees say they lack required skills despite unprecedented access to programs. We've built a $370+ billion industry that produces activity more reliably than capability.

2. **AI has erased the justification for most traditional training.** When learners can ask AI for step-by-step guidance tailored to their context, the rationale for pre-packaged workshops collapses. Research from MIT's Teaching Systems Lab and other groups studying AI-augmented learning suggests that simple, actionable prompts and just-in-time guidance can speed up skill acquisition and improve retention compared with traditional e-learning.

3. **Real learning has always been voluntary, emotional, and messy.** We don't remember what we're forced to sit through; we remember what shook us or helped us survive real problems. Research shows that without emotional relevance, very little sticks. Yet most training is designed around content coverage, not emotional ignition.

Once you accept these realities, the old playbook isn't fixable. It has to be replaced.

The Control Paradox

The greatest barrier isn't technological—it's psychological.

For decades, organizations derived comfort from the illusion that structured training provided control. Everyone attended the same workshop, received the same content, completed the same assessment.

The metrics reinforced the illusion: 94% completion rates, 4.2/5.0 satisfaction scores, 47,000 training hours delivered.

But control over training activity never equaled control over learning outcomes. We controlled attendance while actual learning happened elsewhere—at midnight on YouTube, through trial and error on real problems.

The revolution requires releasing the fantasy that learning can be controlled and accepting it can only be catalyzed.

> The question isn't "How do we ensure everyone learns this?" but "How do we create conditions where people choose to learn what they need?"

What Letting Go Actually Means

"Letting go" sounds abstract. In practice, it's brutally concrete:

From mandatory to market-tested. If a program can't attract voluntary participation, it shouldn't exist. Attendance becomes a signal, not a requirement.

From content ownership to curiosity architecture. L&D's value becomes "we designed the moment that made people care"—not "we built the program." SPARK Sessions embody this: short, intense experiences that provoke emotion and send people down their own rabbit holes.

From LMS-centric to ecosystem-centric. Curate an ecosystem of AI assistants, peer communities, curated resources, and just-in-time nudges. L&D's role becomes orchestration, not manufacture.

From activity metrics to performance evidence. The only metrics that matter are behavior changes, quality of work, time-to-competence, and contribution to outcomes leaders care about.

From central control to shared responsibility. Learning is co-owned by individuals who make choices, managers who create conditions, AI tools that provide guidance, and learning professionals who architect pivotal experiences.

2 Pathways. Your Choice: Evolution or Extinction

PATH ONE: DEFEND THE CASTLE

Continue building better content, improving delivery. This offers comfort and preserves roles. It also guarantees irrelevance.

PATH TWO: LEAD THE REVOLUTION

Abandon control. Stop delivering comprehensive content and start igniting curiosity. Replace extensive programs with compressed experiences designed to provoke questions. The revolution succeeds because it aligns with how humans learn: driven by need, fueled by curiosity, enabled by access when motivation peaks.

What Replaces "Training"

The center of gravity moves toward different defaults:

SPARK-style ignition sessions. Two-hour experiences that surface mental models and activate curiosity—followed by AI-supported exploration and real-work application.

AI as first responder. When someone is stuck, the default becomes "ask the AI copilot." The human layer focuses on meaning-making and judgment.

Managers as learning multipliers. Run stretch assignments, debriefs, peer coaching, and live problem-solving where learning and performance are inseparable.

Learning paths that emerge from problems. When facing real challenges, the "path" becomes a flexible mix of AI guidance, curated resources, and catalytic human experiences.

Over time, "training" becomes smaller. The bigger question: How fast can our people get better at work that matters, using every tool available?

What Leaders Must Do

Transform one program. Redesign one initiative as a SPARK Session. Enable AI follow-through. Measure behavior change.

Make something optional. Make one high-profile program voluntary. The truth about value will emerge quickly.

Enable unmonitored AI access. Give people permission to learn through AI. In one widely cited case study, IBM reported a large increase in employee-initiated learning after rolling out an AI-powered learning platform—without mandating course completions.

Shift your dashboard. Move from activity metrics to performance indicators.

Reward facilitation over expertise. The most valuable capability is provoking curiosity and creating conditions for exploration.

The Cost of Holding On

What if you don't evolve? At first, not much. Dashboards look reassuring. Teams stay busy. But underneath: Your best people bypass formal programs. Critical skills are built through self-directed AI use you don't support. Leaders question why budgets remain high while capability gaps persist. AI-native competitors develop talent faster and cheaper.

Extinction isn't dramatic. It's gradual irrelevance: L&D becomes the department everyone thanks and no one needs.

The Choice

The learning revolution is happening with or without L&D's participation. Employees are already learning through AI. The question is whether L&D evolves into architects of curiosity, or becomes outdated infrastructure everyone works around. Revolutions start with people who stop pretending. Someone finally says what everyone suspects: "This isn't working—and AI has removed our last excuse."

You can lead this transition. You can prove properly designed learning becomes something people seek rather than endure. But only if you let go of what doesn't work. The research is clear. The technology exists. The approaches have been tested. The only missing ingredient is willingness to abandon the familiar. AI won't wait. Employees won't keep pretending training works while AI demonstrates learning can be immediate, personalized, and effective.

> ## The choice was always binary:
> ## Evolution or extinction.

When your employees think about where they learn the most that actually helps them do their jobs better, will your organization even be on that list?

If not, what are you willing to let go of—today—to change that?

CONCLUSION

The Death and The Rebirth of Learning

Why the end of training as we know it is the beginning of learning as it should be

If you've made it this far, you've sat with uncomfortable truths. You've seen the evidence that what we've built doesn't work the way we claimed. You've confronted the systems we've defended, the metrics we've celebrated, and the assumptions we've rarely questioned.

> That discomfort? It's not the end of something. It's the beginning.

Because here's what we've actually been talking about for twelve essays: *liberation*.

Liberation from the pretense that learning happens on our schedules, follows our curriculums, or fits our measurement frameworks. Liberation from the exhausting performance of certainty—the dashboards, the completion rates, the satisfaction scores that assured us we were doing something important while people quietly learned elsewhere.

Liberation to do what we always hoped we were doing: *helping people become genuinely better at work that matters.*

What We're Really Losing

The death of training-as-we-know-it means letting go of control, predictability, and the comfortable illusion that learning is something we do *to* people. It means abandoning the industrial model that treated humans like products on an assembly line, all requiring the same inputs delivered at the same pace.

> That's not a tragedy. That's *overdue.*

What made sense in an era of information scarcity—when organizations genuinely had to centralize and standardize access to knowledge—has become actively harmful in an era of information abundance. We kept building fortresses after the walls became obsolete.

What We're Really Gaining

But look at what becomes possible when we let go:

Learning that starts not with someone else's agenda, but with genuine curiosity sparked in a moment of provocation. Questions that pull people down rabbit holes because they *need* to know, not because they're told to complete. Exploration that happens at 2 AM because someone is genuinely excited about what they're discovering, powered by AI that can meet them exactly where they are.

Managers who stop checking boxes and start creating conditions. Conversations that matter because they're about real challenges, not theoretical scenarios. Experiments that teach more in an afternoon than workshops teach in a week. AI assistants that provide answers when motivation peaks, not weeks later when the need has passed.

And perhaps most important: people who stop seeing learning as something that happens to them in scheduled programs and start experiencing it as something they *drive* in pursuit of becoming better at what they do.

> This is learning as it should be. As it always was, *before we tried to industrialize it*.

The Opportunity Before Us

The AI era hasn't created this crisis—it's simply removed our last excuse for ignoring it.

For years, we could argue that centralized training was necessary because employees couldn't access expertise on demand, couldn't practice skills adaptively, couldn't get immediate feedback on their thinking. Those arguments are gone. The scarcity that justified the system has evaporated.

> What remains is an extraordinary opportunity: *to redesign learning around how humans actually get better at things*.

Not through mandated attendance, but through **ignited curiosity**. Not through comprehensive coverage, but through provocative experiences that make people desperate to learn more. Not through content delivery, but through conditions that make exploration irresistible and application inevitable.

The L.I.Y. Method, SPARK Sessions, AI-enabled ecosystems—these aren't gimmicks. They're experiments in treating adults like the self-directed learners they become the moment something genuinely matters to them. These essays have offered up possibilities and I am the first to admit that implementing the ideas suggested here are easier said than done. The goal never was to offer "guaranteed" solutions but instead to sprinkle some seeds of ideas that could be built upon by the industry—*it is truly okay to fail while trying instead of not trying at all*. The industry is filled with far more capable and brilliant people than I can ever hope to be, and if any of these essays have ignited in them some ideas, possibilities, and a desire to try something different, then this collection of essays has accomplished far more than its goal.

What Happens Next

You have a choice that previous generations of learning professionals didn't have: you can see clearly that the old model is dying, and you can choose to lead what replaces it rather than defend what doesn't work.

This doesn't require perfection. It requires honesty. Honesty about what's not working. Honesty about what AI makes possible. Honesty about how people actually learn when we stop forcing them into systems designed for organizational convenience rather than human curiosity.

Start with one program. Make something optional. Redesign something as a SPARK Session. Enable AI access without oversight. Measure something that matters instead of something that's easy to track.

Not everything at once. Just something that signals you've stopped pretending and started experimenting.

The Beginning

> The death of training as we know it isn't something to mourn. It's something to celebrate.

Because on the other side of this death is a rebirth: learning that feels less like compliance and more like discovery. Development that happens in the flow of work rather than separate from it. Growth that's measured not by hours logged but by capabilities gained and applied.

Imagine a future where the question isn't "Did they complete the training?" but "Are they getting better at work that matters—and do they have everything they need to keep growing?"

Imagine learning and development teams who are celebrated not for the number of programs delivered, but for the moments of curiosity sparked, the rabbit holes that led to breakthroughs, and the capabilities that measurably improved.

Imagine employees who actually look forward to learning opportunities because they know from experience that something genuinely useful, genuinely interesting, genuinely transformative awaits.

That future doesn't require permission. It requires courage.

The courage to let go of what's familiar and build what works. The courage to admit that control was always an illusion and curiosity is what we should have been architecting all along.

The courage to believe that when we stop treating adults like children who need to be managed through standardized programs, and start treating them like the hungry, curious, capable people they actually are, something extraordinary becomes possible.

> The training industrial complex is dying.
> Good. Let it.

Because what comes next—if we're brave enough to build it—isn't just better training.

It's learning as it should be. As it always wanted to be. And that beginning starts with you.

What will you let go of—today—to make space for what comes next?

Shaurav Sen

Dubai | Washington D.C. | Singapore | New Delhi

Let's Connect and Continue:

*How to Take These Conversations
Deeper with Your Team*

> If these essays resonated—if they surfaced
> questions you've been wrestling with or challenged
> assumptions you didn't realize you were making—
> the conversation doesn't have to end here.

After 32 years of making work the priority, I've made a deliberate choice to focus on things I'd made secondary for too long—family, travel, personal interests. I'm not looking to replace my corporate career with another version of the same thing. But I am open to thoughtful engagements with people genuinely exploring these ideas, as long as they fit within the balance I'm trying to create.

That's why what follows is structured the way it is. I want to be honest about what I can offer and realistic about my availability. If that sounds like it might align with what you're looking for, here are a few ways we might work together.

VIRTUAL BRIEFINGS:
Unpacking the book
(75 minutes, virtual)

These are straightforward conversations where I walk your team through key insights from the book and we explore how they might—or might not—apply to your context. It's not a sales call. It's a chance to pressure-test these ideas against your specific challenges.

Before we schedule, I'll ask you to share what you're trying to address and which parts of the book felt most relevant. That helps ensure we're both using our time well. If there's no clear fit, I'll tell you honestly.

What you get: 75 minutes of focused conversation. What you don't get: a pitch for follow-on work or pressure to adopt any particular approach.

EXECUTIVE BRIEFINGS:
For Strategy Offsites
(2.5 hours, in-person)

For executive teams or leadership offsites where there's genuine openness to rethinking your approach to learning, an in-person session creates space for deeper exploration.

The first hour focuses on core insights from the book, grounded in your organization's actual dilemmas. The remaining time is interactive—surfacing possibilities and helping your team ask better questions of each other.

The real value isn't my presentation—it's the conversation it sparks among your own team. These work best when leadership is prepared for honest discussion about what's working and what isn't.

Pricing reflects time plus at-cost travel.

SOUNDING BOARD SESSIONS:
Applying SPARK
(virtual, short-term)

If you read Essay 11 on the SPARK Framework and want help thinking through how to apply it to something you're building, I'm happy to serve as a sounding board.

I won't redesign your program or create materials—you do the work. But I'll provide specific suggestions on how SPARK principles might reshape what you're developing. These are short engagements (3-5 hours total, virtual) spread over a few days.

Speaking Engagements
(conferences, events)

I'm open to speaking opportunities where these ideas might provoke useful conversations for larger audiences. These need to be scheduled well in advance given other commitments, and I'll want to understand why this audience and what you hope might shift as a result.

A Note on What This Isn't

Given where I am in my life, I'm not looking to build a traditional consulting practice. I won't propose long-term engagements or try to convince anyone to adopt a particular system. The ideas in this book are yours to use or adapt as you see fit. If we work together, it's to help you think more clearly—not to create an ongoing dependency.

This selective approach isn't about being exclusive—it's about being *realistic*. I want to work with people and teams where there's genuine mutual interest in exploring these ideas, and where the engagement fits within the life balance I'm trying to maintain.

How to Connect

If you'd like to explore whether there's a fit, reach out:

Email: sen@shaurav.org
LinkedIn: linkedin/shauravs
Website: shaurav.org

In your initial message, share what you're trying to address, which parts of the book hit home, and what would make our time together productive. If there's alignment, we'll figure out next steps. If not, I'll be honest and perhaps point you toward other resources.

Final Thought

The ideas in this book don't need me to be useful. But if you want to explore how they might apply to your specific challenges or use them to spark more honest conversations in your team, I'm happy to help—within the limits of what I can reasonably commit to.

The rest is up to you.

APPENDIX
Useful Readings and References

These books, research studies, and industry reports informed the ideas in this book. They offer deeper insights across learning science, behavior change, organizational culture, and the future of work.

Learning Science & Cognitive Psychology

Ebbinghaus, H. (1913). Memory: A Contribution to Experimental Psychology. Teachers College Press.

Murre, J. M. J., & Dros, J. (2015). "Replication and Analysis of Ebbinghaus' Forgetting Curve." PLOS ONE, 10(7).

Bjork, R. A., & Bjork, E. L. (2011). "Desirable Difficulties." In Psychology of Learning and Motivation, Vol. 55.

Brown, P., Roediger, H. L., & McDaniel, M. (2014). Make It Stick: Why Some Ideas Survive and Others Die. Belknap Press.

Clark, R. C., Nguyen, F., & Sweller, J. (2006). Efficiency in Learning. Wiley.

Tyng, C. M., Amin, H. U., Saad, M. N. M., & Malik, A. S. (2017). "The Influences of Emotion on Learning and Memory." Frontiers in Psychology.

Pane, J. F., Steiner, E. D., Baird, M. D., & Hamilton, L. S. (2017). Informing Progress: Insights on Personalized Learning. RAND Corporation.

Koedinger, K. R., & Nathan, M. J. (2004). "Cognitive Tutors." Encyclopedia of Social and Behavioral Sciences.

Willingham, D. T. (2009). Why Don't Students Like School? Jossey-Bass.

Privitera, A. J. (2023). "Defining the Science of Learning: A Scoping Review." Educational Research Review.

Asadullah, M., Yeasmin, M., Alam, A. F., et al. (2023). "A Systematic Review of Mobile Learning in Higher Education." Sustainability, 15(17), 12847.

Adult Learning, Pedagogy & Instructional Design

Knowles, M. S. (2015). The Adult Learner (8th ed.). Routledge.

Shulman, L. S. (1986). "Those Who Understand: Knowledge Growth in Teaching." Educational Researcher, 15(2).

Wieman, C. E. (2017). Improving How Universities Teach Science. Harvard University Press.

Perry, T., et al. (2022). *A decade of replication study in education? A mapping review (2011-2020).* Educational Research Review, 34, Article 100431.

Ambrose, S. A., Bridges, M. W., DiPietro, M., Lovett, M. C., & Norman, M. K. (2010). How Learning Works. Jossey-Bass.

Behavior, Motivation & Habit Formation

Fogg, B. J. (2020).
Tiny Habits. Morrow.

Heath, C., & Heath, D. (2007).
Made to Stick. Random House.

Pink, D. H. (2009).
Drive. Riverhead Books.

Ryan, R. M., & Deci, E. L. (2017).
Self-Determination Theory.
Guilford Press.

Shanteau, J. (1992).
"Competence in Experts: The
Role of Task Characteristics."
Organizational Behavior and
Human Decision Processes, 53.

Kahneman, D. (2011).
Thinking, Fast and Slow.
Farrar, Straus and Giroux.

Duckworth, A. (2016).
Grit. Scribner.

Baumeister, R., & Tierney, J. (2011).
Willpower. Penguin.

Organizational Behavior, Culture & Change

Kotter, J. P. (1996).
Leading Change.
Harvard Business Review Press.

Schein, E. H. (2016).
Organizational Culture &
Leadership (5th ed.). Wiley.

Sutton, R. I., & Rao, H. (2014).
Scaling Up Excellence.
Crown Business.

Newport, C. (2016).
Deep Work.
Grand Central Publishing.

Argyris, C., & Schön, D. (1978).
Organizational Learning.
Addison-Wesley.

Senge, P. (1990).
The Fifth Discipline.
Doubleday.

Workplace Learning, Talent & Future of Work

Association for Talent Development. State of the Industry (Annual Reports).

Deloitte. Global Human Capital Trends (Annual Reports).

LinkedIn Learning. Workplace Learning Report (Annual Reports).

Corporate Leadership Council (CEB/Gartner). (2004). Driving Performance and Retention Through Employee Engagement.

NeuroLeadership Institute. AGES Model Resources.

MIT Teaching Systems Lab. Teaching & AI Research Resources.

Gallup. State of the Global Workplace (Annual Reports).

Microsoft. Work Trend Index (Annual Reports).

World Economic Forum. (2023). The Future of Jobs Report.

McKinsey Global Institute. (2024). A New Future of Work: The Race to Deploy AI and Raise Skills.